A MODEL OF MAKING: LITERARY CRITICISM AND ITS THEOLOGY

Other titles in the series

A MODEL OF MAKING: LITERARY CRITICISM AND ITS THEOLOGY

RUTH ETCHELLS

MARSHALL MORGAN & SCOTT

Marshall Morgan & Scott
3 Beggarwood Lane, Basingstoke, Hants., UK.

ISBN 0 551 01020 7

Printed in Great Britain by Intergraphic (UK) Ltd

In memory of my mother

ADA ETCHELLS

1889 – 1981

whose patience helped to shape
this book

Contents

Acknowledgements

This study has been a long time in the making, and even now would not have emerged without the very considerable help of a number of people. I would particularly like to thank the Revd. Dr. Paul Avis, General Editor, for assistance in structuring it; Professor Emeritus Ulrich Simon and Dr. J. W. Dillistone for much stimulation and guidance; Miss Marjorie Cooper and Miss Margaret Jack for careful scrutiny and much valuable comment; my colleague, the Revd. Dr. Bruce Kaye, for undertaking much extra work during my own sabbatical leave and thus freeing me to revise the text very thoroughly; and Mrs. Doris Kay, secretary extraordinary, who can do everything, including making sense of my handwriting.

D. R. E.

October 1982.
St. John's College, Durham.

Prologue

The style of literary criticism which held sway most strongly through a large part of the twentieth century was that of the liberal humanist, detached and objective, arguing no partisan approach, asserting that the personal values of the critics were irrelevant. What was not allowed for, of course, was that this view was itself an expression of values – those of tolerance and, above all, objectivity.

The critical scene is now very different, with many disparate styles of critical enterprise based on varying and distinctive world views: those of the Marxist or the linguistic philosopher, for instance. Each brings an individual and highly characteristic perspective to the critical activity.

This being the case, it is timely, not least in view of the Christian roots of Western civilisation, to further the discussion of what might be the characteristics and insights of a specifically Christian criticism. Such a criticism must have a theological grounding. That is, it must attempt not the inferring of Christian belief or theme in writers who will in most cases be non-Christian; but rather the exploring of the creative laws, under which writers operate, as they might be understood both by a critic and a Christian theologian.

So this book is intended to promote such discussion. It examines what is the writer's activity as 'maker', as some writers have understood it; as some critics have understood it; and as theologians might perceive it. Such conclusions as it offers grow, ultimately, from the breadth and richness that emerge as available when we consider the 'model of making' that God himself offers as Creator; a model for both writers and critics – and perhaps theologians as well? – in their own particular making.

Every voyage is a death
Every action is a loss
Every poem drees its weird
Carries its meaning like a cross.
Yet the burnt poet loves the fire
Which gulps what pittance he can give
Dry words dying, dying dead,
Burning that the Word may live!

(W. H. Auden, Preface to
Ten Burnt Offerings)

CHAPTER ONE

Introduction

It is not often that the ways of literary critics become a matter of such widespread interest as to rate columns in the national (daily) press. Yet such has been the case quite recently. Though on the whole there was little popular interest in the causes of dissension which had created such a furore among the academics, there was surprised recognition that here were matters of such moment to those involved that they generated the sort of passions others attach to patriotism or ideologies or religious faith. What the nation generally was noting was, of course, the mere glint of helmets in the distance. It is unlikely that many recognised the strength and force of the armies engaged, or that what was at issue was revolution; a revolution whose implications reached far wider than the literary critical departments which provided the cockpit.

For literary criticism has to do with literature, and with the task and responsibility of writers; and it also has to do with the climate of ideas within any age, and with matters of faith, and commitment, with philosophical world views and with social ideologies. It concerns itself with what a writer is doing when he is writing, and thence with what is the nature of art. It also concerns itself with what kind of a 'reality' that art is registering, and in so doing it raises questions which are often political, often social, often philosophical, as well as necessarily aesthetic. Sometimes, indeed very frequently, these questions also concern belief; insofar as the category is admitted at all, religious belief. Indeed, it is arguable that at root that is what much of the debate is most fundamentally about.

This is no new situation of course. It is now just over a century since the relationship of literary criticism to biblical studies became part of a theological revolution. Yet by now that relationship has become so much a part of biblical exegesis that it has, so to speak, merged into the background of the more general discussion of principles. Dame Helen Gardner, in her book *The Business of Criticism*[1], did well, therefore, to remind us first of how revolutionary the discovery of this relationship had seemed, and second, of its continuing importance in the second half of the twentieth century. She quoted Charles Gore's words in *Lux Mundi* (1889):

> 'A literary criticism is being developed, which is as really new an intellectual product as the scientific development and, as such, certain to reverse a good many of the literary judgments of previous ages.'[2]

and she went on to assert that it was still true that 'developments in literary criticism and the problems they raise are . . . of concern to those who hold the Christian faith'. At the point at which Dame Helen gave the lectures which are the substance of that book[3], the emphasis was still, as it had been in the previous century, primarily on the insights which the disciplines of literary criticism could bring to the understanding of the Christian faith. But since the middle of the twentieth century there has been a growing awareness of the way in which this relationship between the two disciplines can become more fully mutual by taking account also of the illumination which theologians can bring to the activity of literary criticism.

This mutuality of relationship between the two disciplines seems to be regarded as just as radical and controversial as the earlier disputes over whether the techniques of literary criticism could properly be applied to the biblical text, and it has been attended by much the same opprobrium, this time from literary rather than theological scholars. Yet it has become increasingly clear that the insights of modern theologians could be particularly important for an understanding of the craft of writing and its attendant criticism, at this present time. And conversely, that contemporary critical thought has something of great value to offer theologians and biblical scholars. It is to this mutuality that this book is addressed.

The rejection of traditional cricitism

The ferment in which literary critics find themselves is, I suspect, greater than at any point since the Romantic revolution. We may begin by glancing at M. H. Abrams's famous identification of critical approaches, a summary which we shall look at in much more detail later. Abrams records that most past critical disputes have arisen from an overwhelming emphasis on one, more than on any of the other three, of the four elements which are essential to almost all critical theories which aim to be comprehensive:

'First, there is the *work*, the artistic product itself. And since this is a human product, an artefact, the second common element is the artificer, the *artist*. Third, the work is taken to have a subject, which is derived from existing things. . . – an objective state of affairs. (For) this third element ,. . let us use the . . . comprehensive term, *universe*. For the final element we have the *audience*: the listeners, spectators or readers to whom the work is addressed, or to whose attention . . . it becomes available. . .
. . . Although any reasonably adequate theory takes some account of all four elements, almost all theories . . . exhibit a discernible orientation towards one only.'[4]

These views seem almost inarguable in their obviousness. Yet it is not a 'discernible orientation towards one only' of these elements in a work of art which is breaking open the groundwork of literary criticism. Rather I think it would be true to say that the work (for instance) of Roland Barthes and fellow structuralists and of Saussure whose semiotics Barthes follows, would largely repudiate significance in Abrams's 'four elements'; would indeed call into question the whole critical enterprise as hitherto understood, rejecting any distinction between the creative work and the critical commentary on it, and arguing;

> 'The task of criticism is not to discover forms of truth, but forms of "validity. . ." if there is such a thing as critical proof, it lies not in the ability to *discover* the work under consideration but, on the contrary, to cover it as completely as possible with one's own language.'[5]

And therefore, as Eugenio Donato comments, instead of a creative work and its concomitant, a critical commentary,

> 'what we have is language and the single problematic it imposes, that of interpreatation. . . If. . . linguistic signs refer themselves only to other linguistic signs, if the linguistic reference of words is words, if texts refer to nothing but other texts, then, in Foucault's words, "If interpretation can never accomplish itself, it is simply because there is nothing to interpret." '[6]

In other words, all writing, critical and creative, is 'nothing but structure', nothing 'but the infinity of its own envelopes, no heart, no kernel, no secret.' 'Subject' is an 'illusory notion'.[7] Communication – of the universe, of the artist, of the reader – is 'not at the heart of the linguistic act but only an epiphenomenon':

> 'If literature tells a story, if the author has to use a reference, it is simply a consequence of the fact that he is manipulating a linguistic sign.'[8]

That is, there is no communication and *there is nothing to communicate*.

The imperialism of an ideology

Behind this view of literature as having no reference beyond itself, and as being of no significance within itself except as a pattern of 'structures' lies a view of the universe and a value judgment concerning it. 'It is difficult', David Lodge writes, 'to see how the argument could be profitably continued without moving from the area of literature, and criticism to that of philosophy'[9] since:

> 'not only does semiotic formalism seek to abolish the referential function of language in literary texts, a function in ordinary language. . . .; it also denies the epistemological validity of empiricism and the concept of the unique, autonomous self-conscious individual.'[10]

Catherine Belsey goes further. Reviewing not only semiotics, but some of these approaches to criticism which suggest that literature is either the solvent for the 'class struggle', or the context in which that struggle must be furthered, she concludes:

> 'No theoretical position can exist in isolation: any conceptual framework for literary criticism has implications which stretch beyond criticism itself to ideology and the place of ideology in the social formation as a whole. Assumptions about literature involve assumptions about language and about meaning, and these in turn involve assumptions about human society. The independent universe of literature and the autonomy of criticism are illusory.'[11]

Certainly it seems no longer possible to take an ideologically neutral position in postulating a basis to the critical study of literature. (By 'ideology' I mean, as Ms. Belsey does, 'not an optional extra, deliberately adopted by self-conscious individuals. . . . but the very condition of our experience of the world'.[12]) Dame Helen Gardner, on the occasion already referred to, had already made the same point, rather more tranquilly: 'The critic's attitude to works of art must depend ultimately on his conception of the nature of man.'[13] The revolutionaries have at the very least established that no critical perceptions are ideologically pure, that our 'recognition' and evaluation of works of literature is inevitably to some degree culturally conditioned. They have also established (largely by denigration) that any ideology offered as a base for criticism must be adequate to the whole range of questions which are implicit in the critical enterprise, without the support of hidden assumptions. Such contributions to the debate are radical and valuable.

The potential of a Christian 'ideology'

But the ideological offering put before us is arid, abstract and dehumanising. It explicitly rejects the value of the individual and his uniqueness; and, just as significantly, it finds no place for the notion of 'dynamos', the power which compels the artist; what I suppose would be called by Coleridge 'the Imagination'. We shall be looking further at this in due course. What I would suggest here is that such a critical approach – which in its aggressive imperialism brooks no alternatives or complementary views – is itself inadequate, in its own formulations, to the full range of those human experiences which all great art signals. And in saying so I would suggest further that a Christian humanistic ideology be re-examined, as a live option rather than as a derelict framework whose usefulness is long past.

To speak of a Christian 'ideology' is in the first place to speak of its theology, for it is from the depth, range and vitality of its underlying theology that a Christian ideology can prove itself adequate to the critical questions at issue. Hence a need to explore some aspects of the writer's creative activity as it might be understood in the light of a theological model. If such a theological 'grounding' of the writer's creative act is available and proves itself able to accommodate such questions as the new radical critics, or the 'formalists', are raising, then we have here a way of approaching literature exposed by the shaking of foundations they have caused, but in no way dominated or over-ruled by them.

The contemporary writer's diagnostic role

I see the need for such a study as urgent, not only because of the present instability of critical practice, but more par-

ticularly because of the peculiar context within which the
contemporary artist creates his work. It is not just that this
is an age of 'unfaith': indeed, that is so to over-simplify the
character of the age as to be an almost meaningless description
of it. Rather, it is the particular pressure upon the writer by
the contemporary public to fulfil a prophetic or a diagnostic
role which makes the theologian's comments of some relevance. Saul Bellow has well expressed the dilemma of many
modern writers in a passage to be found in one of his short
stores:

'To understand . . . . you have to think first of modern
literature as a sort of grand council considering what mankind
should do next, how we should fill our mortal time, what we
should feel, where we should get our courage, how we should
love or hate, how we should be pure or great or terrible, evil
(you know!) and all the rest. This advice of literature has never
done much good. But you see, God doesn't rule over men as he
used to, and for a long time people haven't been able to feel
that life was firmly attached at both ends so that they could
confidently stand in the middle. That kind of faith is missing,
and for many years poets have tried to supply a substitute. Like
the "unacknowledged legislators" or "the best is yet to be" or
Walt Whitman saying that whoever touched him could be sure
he was touching a man. Some have stood up for beauty and
some have stood up for perfect proportion, and the very best
have soon gotten tired of art for its own sake. Some took it as
their duty to behave like brave performers who try to hold
down panic during a theatre fire. Very great ones have quit,
like Tolstoy who becomes a reformer, or like Rimbaud, who
went to Abyssinia, and at the end of his life was begging of a
priest, "Montrez-moi. Montrez. . . Show me something."
Frightening, the lives some of these genuises led. Maybe they
assumed too much responsibility. They knew that if by their
poems and novels *they* were fixing values, there must be
something wrong with the values. No one man can furnish
them. Oh, he may try, if his inspiration is for values, but not if
his inspiration is for words. If you throw the full responsiblity
for meaning and for the establishing of good and evil on poets

they are bound to go down. However, the poets reflected what
was happening to everyone.'[14]

It is partly because many writers are in some sense 'establishing good and evil', because they have thrust upon them
'responsibility for meaning' (or the assertion of its opposite),
because they have tried and are trying to supply a 'substitue
for faith', that the theologian cannot properly avoid response
and comment. We might remember Wallace Steven's
comment:

'In an age of disbelief . . . it is for the poet to supply the
satisfactions of belief. . . I think of it as a role of the utmost
seriousness. It is, for one thing, a spiritual role. . . In an age of
disbelief, when the gods have come to an end . . . men turn to
a fundamental glory of their own and from that create a style of
bearing themselves in reality.'[5]

Moreover, the artist today, even if he disclaims the determining or even identifying of good and evil, can be faced with
a demand for universality which adds to his responsibility. In
his Nobel Prize speech, *One Word of Truth*, it was this role of
the writer, beyond all others, which Alexander Solzhenitsyn
urged. It was not so much that a writer must establish indi-
vidually the meaning of life, of good and evil, as that by the
work of poets, playwrights, novelists, there could be brought
to bear upon the whole of the reading world, in every part of
the globe, the reality of good and evil as each nation in its
own catastrophic history had discovered it: so that there
should be available for mankind communally not only the
shared discoveries of all scientists, but the shared knowledge
of the morally and spiritually experienced:

'Who will create for mankind a single system of evaluation – for
evil deeds and good deeds, for what is intolerable, for how the
line is to be drawn between them today?. . . Who would be
able to bring home to a bigoted and obstinate human being the
distant grief and joy of other people, the understanding of

relationships and misconceptions that he himself has never experienced? Propaganda, compulsion and scientific proof are all powerless here. But fortunately the means to convey all this to us does exist in the world. It is Art. It is literature. Art and literature can perform the miracle of overcoming man's characteristic weakness of learning only by his own experience, so that the experience of others passes him by. . . Art re-creates in the flesh all experience lived by other men, so that each man can make this his own . . . .

Even more, much more than this: countries, whole continents, repeat each other's mistakes at a later date, sometimes centuries later, when one would have thought everything was so painfully obvious. But no! What some peoples have already experienced, thought out and rejected is suddenly discovered by others as the very last word. Here again, the only thing that can take the place of experience we have not lived is Art, literature. They provide a miraculous facility: that of overcoming differences of language, custom and social system, and conveying one whole nation to another. And this national experience, painfully built up over many decades by one nation, when conveyed to a second nation which has never had it, can perhaps save it from taking an unnecessary, mistaken or even ruinous path. Thus Art can somewhat straighten the twisted paths of man's history.'[16]

Such a view lays upon writers the task not of creating, but extending, across the world normative values by which each nation shall judge itself, and be judged.

The shared task

Both these claims for and demands on the writer seem to me to lay upon the literary artist, the critic and the theologian the necessity of a shared labour; for the demand that contemporary writers should act as 'prophets' arises from the dislocation of values normative to reader, writer and critic. We have, for instance, to ask ourselves – artist, critic, theologian – what we mean by the terms 'creating' and 'judging'. Our view of these terms *in the context of art* will be shaped by our conception of man, and whether we understand his powers to be those of the creature standing in relation to a particular kind of Creator or otherwise. Similarly, our acceptance of the deliberate disjunction currently adumbrated between the artist's 'creating' and the reader's 'assessing' or 'judging' may be sharply modified by what the theologian has to say of the relation between 'creation' and 'judgment'.

There is one further aspect of the task before us which I would like to highlight here. It has to do with the relation between a Christian literary criticism and a theology of criticism. Leland Ryken has commented with some anxiety about the confusion between the two:

> 'The time has come for literary critics to insist on the difference between Christian literary criticism and theological criticism in literature.'[17]

and he attacks with passion 'the inability to treat literature as anything other than religion (just as sociologists and psychologists find it hard to treat literature as anything besides sociology and psychology.)'

Professor Ryken is quite right to attack the use of literature for theological exposition *under the name of literary criticism*. But it is entirely proper for the theologian to perceive how some piece of creative writing illuminates the theological proposition with which he has been struggling, provided he does not call this illumination 'criticism'. Indeed, such a mutual exchange between the disciplines is valuable to both, provided it is recognised as exchange and not as the one and the same activity.

But having given this full assent, one would wish to make sure that in safeguarding these proper activities we did not lose sight of the need to establish a common framework. Christian literary criticism can only function *at all* if its theological base (and it cannot exist as *Christian* without one) is thought-out and established within whatever is the contemporary critical debate. Therefore a 'theology of criticism' must underline and even pre-date the enterprise of Christian critical activity. Once that is to some extent a 'given', then the Christian critic can get on with his task in its own proper methodology. But if he does not confront the current maelstrom of critical ideologies, his comments will become increasingly irrelevant to the continuance of critical perception, a lonely trumpeter who has not noticed that the army to which he was giving direction has marched away, leaving him irrelevant and alone on the dusty plain. The function of the Christian critic is to criticise, not to theologise: but to do the one he *must have done* the other.

Outline proposals

It is against this background that this book has been written. It is an essay in an area that others like Giles Gunn[18] are also exploring though not precisely in this form. The works of Nathan Scott, Amos Wilder, David Anderson, John Lawlor, Ulrich Simon and Martin Jarrett-Kerr, to name but a few, have very thoroughly opened up some of its implications. In this study I have been trying to discover what are the roots of such inter-disciplinary analysis, at a rather more fundamental level than I have so far touched on. In particular, I want to begin from the Christian's credal affirmation of 'One God. . . maker of heaven and earth, of all that is, seen and unseen.'[19] What does this statement imply about God as 'maker', both for the critical appraisal of literature and for certain insights in theology today? Two questions were in my mind at this point. The first was, whether in that statement there was any illumination, indeed any indication, of a potential critical basis for the study of literature. That is, whether there was here a referrant for a critic's evaluation, something inherent in the very nature of that literary activity which is 'making', which yet pointed *beyond* the literary activity.

The second question, which followed from this, was whether, in proposing such a study, one might be involved in a rediscovery of certain aspects of God the Creator which threw light on contemporary debate, and such terms within

it as 'story' or 'myth'. The artist and critic both have something to say about these terms which are their own and about
the philosophy and technique of language use which lies behind them. Not only are such terms currently applicable to
the christological debate, but conceivably they draw their
deepest meaning from it.

And further, there was here the conjunction of God the
Creator with God the Law Giver and Judge. Every writer
utilises certain basic laws of creative energy in his 'making',
modified by the nature of his material, that of words. 'Law',
therefore, is a concept he acknowledges (though he might
prefer to call it 'structure'). But the nature of that law is in
artistic and critical dispute. The theologian, for his part, is
also interested, though from a different perspective, in concepts of 'creation' and 'judgment'. A rationale for some of the
insights which theologians, writers and critics can offer each
other may well be identifiable in this area.

I propose, therefore, to look at the two modes of making
presented to us: that which the writer (and hence the literary
critic) understands of his own: that which the theologian
suggests, both about God's making and man's. I want to see
at what points there are analogies, if any, and how these
analogies might be understood. That leads us on to ask if the
theological model can suggest insights germane to the literary
one, and, vice versa, what insights we might gain theologically
through the literary and linguistic models available.

Beyond these critical questions, of course, lie other, inter-
pretative ones. What have theologians to say of dereliction?
or of joy? – two of the most constantly explored themes in
contemporary writing, though they appear not under those
names but as loss, deprivation, loneliness, despair, grieving,
alienation, annihilation, on the one hand, and on the other as
security, enlargement, ecstasy, loving. In a book of this kind
it has been possible only to glance obliquely at such issues,
though where possible I have used contemporary literature to
help clarify critical ideas. I have tried also to indicate here
and there where such writing illuminates or is illuminated by

the insights which present-day theologians are offering. In doing so, I am well aware of one of the gravest dangers of such a proceeding: that of equating like with unlike, of so transcribing from one category into another that both are falsified. To suggest that all writers and critics are 'Christian' in some sense because all of them are engaged in an activity for which there is, finally, a Christian model, is manifestly absurd.[20] To suggest that profoundly 'Christian' views are expressed by writers who are explicitly atheist can come very near this absurdity, and is rightly fiercely rejected by them. But there are many writers who do not profess the Christian faith, or specifically reject it, whose concern is with questions of man's innocence and guilt, obedience and sacrifice, belief and doubt, in some ultimate sense. Often these writers have insights which those accepting the Christian faith would find extending or enriching or even frighteningly acute: often they ask questions which probe crucially the kind of statements theologians make.

Since linguistics, or semiology, or semiotics, is so powerful a contender for the ultimate critical perspective, it has seemed not inappropriate to begin this study by looking at word-use. I have approached this initially, however, from populist and artistic usage rather than critical theory. From there it is natural in a study of this kind to relate thinking about human word-use to Logos theology, the doctrine of the creative function of the Word.

Having established these parameters it is then possible to look at the current debate among literary critics, and propose a style of criticism rooted in a Christian ideology, while noting the potential abuse of such a *schema*. And so finally we move to some suggested implications for theologians and critics alike. I have called these 'some conclusions'. Really they are mere beginnings. My hope is that others will see much more fully and more deeply what these 'conclusions' might be, and one day develop them for us.

CHAPTER TWO

Some words and the Word

Verbal transience and the 'old bardic belief'.

In John Osborne's play, *West of Suez*, the central character is a successful, albeit elderly and rather weary writer. From time to time the play concerns itself with what his art and success have amounted to, and very near the end of it Osborne neatly organises a staged 'mass media' interview in which he can make the interviewer ask all the questions on which Osborne wishes to deliver his views. Perhaps one of the most important questions the interviewer asks, in view of what happens at the end of the play, is this:

'In these changing times, do you still believe that words in themselves have any meaning, value or validity?'

The reply is speedy but gnomic:

'I still cling pathetically to the old bardic belief that "words alone are certain good".'[1]

It is valuable to begin a discussion of some aspects of contemporary word-use from this point because John Osborne, for all his dramatic and literary faults, has been an extraordinarily sensitive barometer of western cultural weather; and in this tiny interchange lie some of the basic questions we have to consider. First, there is the importance of the context in which the question is put: 'In these changing times', the questioner begins. That is, our 'today', with its instability of pre-supposition, must affect the meaning, value and validity of words: is this partial or total? Behind this lies, of course, the suggestion that the whole activity of word-using is not a 'given', a necessary element in the definition of what it is to be human; but rather something that is in flux, no longer having unquestionable or undeniable significance in human activity. Indeed, contemporary speculation would contend that 'language teaches the definition of man, not the reverse', since 'man does not exist prior to language, either as a species or as an individual'.[2] Insofar as man is a linguistic being, the drama suggests here that it is no longer possible to assume that this means anything about him that can be agreed upon. The implications of this have been canvassed very fully by both literary and linguistic critics and by anthropologists, and we shall note some of their conclusions in chapter four. Set against this abandonment of stable word referrents, however, is the answer of the writer, the word-spinner, offering 'the old bardic belief that words alone are certain good'.

It is by no means clear what is meant by the use of the word 'alone' in this context, though some of its possible implications emerge later, as we shall see. But 'certain' has the connotation of verity; of the unshakeable, of that which is rooted in some objective reality and therefore unchangeable and not to be diverted. Linked with this is the use of the word 'good', with the notion of 'beneficent' or 'benign' in their many senses.

From a snatch of dialogue in a contemporary play, therefore, it is possible to extrapolate some of the fundamental questions about the nature of this activity of word-using which are currently in debate. The discussion is being generally conducted in language that is often technical and even deliberately and necessarily opaque. The value of using a *dramatic* context for the discussion, as I have chosen to do throughout much of this chapter, rather than a philosophical or critical one, is that it keeps the level of debate that of fairly accessible human daily encounter.

To explore some of the aspects of the question I propose first to look at what a professional and much-praised poet has said about the medium of words, and to study the way she has used words to say it. That is, I have chosen to begin, not from the theoretical speculations of the analyst, but from the descriptive power of the creative artist, the 'maker', the word-spinner. Moving on from what is available there, I want to look at the use of words in everyday, fairly commonplace situations of communication and see how that use seems related to the carefully weighed or imaginatively fired verbal organisation of the 'professional'. Finally, it will be necessary to distinguish between the categories of communication which by then will be emerging. These have implications beyond themselves for a theoretical framework (such as I referred to in chapter one) adequate to the nature of the writing activity and its concomitant critical question. Of the many ideologies currently offered as appropriate perspectives within which the artistic task can be understood, there emerges as valid a theology of criticism which seems to accommodate most of the categories of word-use appearing; as we shall see.

Words as 'tools'.

To begin with the very sensitive appraisal of word-use written by Sylvia Plath, in her poem, 'Words':

WORDS

Axes
After whose stroke the word rings,
And the echoes!
Echoes travelling
Off from the centre like horses.

The sap
Wells like tears, like the
Water striving
To re-establish its mirror

Over the rock
That drops and turns,
A white skull,
Eaten by weedy greens.
Years later I
Encounter them on the road –

Words, dry and riderless,
The indefatigable hoof-taps,
While
From the bottom of the pool, fixed stars
Govern a life.[3]

If we trace the thought in this poem we find that her first concept of words is that of tools, sharp and keen-edged, so handled as to impinge upon, possibly to utilise for the sake of the human race, some natural element which is not easily utilised, manipulated, or shaped. The use of these tools, 'axes', implies effort and precision. The emphasis of the poem immediately moves away from the tools themselves, the words used, to their echoes, their sounds and the reverberations of those sounds. The sounds of the words – i.e. what people hear – almost immediately travel 'off centre' (a careful pun) so that at one and the same time they are further from the original, though presumably heard – with increasingly less truth to the original – by an increasing number of people.

From here the thought develops in two ways. The poet traces the two concepts of how, if at all, the original matter, the natural element, the basic reality, is affected by the thrust and force of these tools; and secondly, she suggests what happens to the words and also what the final value of the activity is: what, if anything, the energetic manipulation of words or reality has achieved. To do this she introduces a second image which, like the first, has to do with the intrusion of the word-shapes upon some primary element, some basic natural reality. This time the image is of a pool into which a rock has been thrown, and she makes the link between the two images firstly by the reference to the sap which 'wells like tears' from the riven tree, and secondly by the movement of the water after the rock or stone has displaced it, which (as we know) ripples outwards in broadening circles just like the echoes travelling off from the centre, as it attempts to re-establish its mirror. The poem concentrates on the development of this image and abandons that of the 'riven tree' except by its inclusion, by implication, in the reference to the words whose echoes were like horses met much later in time. What Sylvia Plath suggests is that however we attempt to make the basic realities which are the context of our life our own, and direct them verbally to our own ends, they are not to be seized upon, and long after the effort is over and the head which initiated such effort (comparable with throwing a rock in a pool) is no more than a white skull eaten by weedy greens, the final natural truth remains unchanged, undisturbed, un-manipulated, governing our lives like 'fixed stars'. The words which were the tools used to attempt this grappling with, and utilisation of, reality are dead. They are like the skull, or at the least diminished in vitality, and wandering, unguided and random, like horses which have become dry and riderless.

So much for the development of the poem. What in sum this poem suggests about the use of words is that, first, they are an attempt to draw upon, to activate, to impinge upon, a reality which is *the* reality of the cosmos insofar as we perceive it: that is why it is expressed in natural terms – tree, water, stars. Secondly, in the immediacy of the effort to use words to grapple with 'reality', those words do take on, in shadowy form, something, some aspect, of the nature of that reality. There is movement, vitality: air and water shake and are disturbed and the words take on the quality of life suggested by that disturbance. But, this quality of vitality and of relation to the reality at the centre is only transient. That is, at best words can only temporarily sustain their expression of reality: and this is because they are tools, objects; with no life in themselves but only in their use.[4] I think the importance of this latter point makes it necessary to underline it, since, as we shall see, there is an important distinction to be made between this understanding of 'words', with a lower case 'w', and the understanding we shall see emerging later in another writer, of Word with a capital 'W'. So in this poem, even for a poet words have no sustained life in themselves. They are objects, and the vitality which attaches to them is somehow connected with their *use*, with the sharpness and force with which they open up whatever ultimate reality is.

There is an important distinction to be made between the view of transience in language put forward in this poem and the view I quoted earlier, implied in the phrase 'in these changing times'. In Sylvia Plath's poem 'reality' remains entirely unchanging, unplumbed and continuous in nature. It is the *words* which lose their currency, dependent as they are on changing 'use' for their vitality.

There is something else that must be said about the use of words as it appears in this poem. That is, that they are being used to communicate the problem of the uncommunicable. The poet is handling words in such a way as to suggest powerfully the problems inherent in handling words. The communicating power of words in this poem depends on several factors, which, as we shall see, are variously essential to words in the communication process at almost every level. One such factor is that the poet must focus our attention and make some of her meaning clear to us, communicate it, that is, in a sharp and well-defined way, by certain key words which are ones of concreteness and particularity: as in the poem we have examined appear, 'axes', 'horses', 'wood', 'rock', 'water', 'road', 'pool': that which is natural in life.

But these are held in tension with others whose edges are blurred, whose usage is suggestive rather than defining, meant to point the imagination beyond itself to some vast background rather than distinguish sharply the foreground object. Such words are 'echoes', 'travelling', 'stirring', 'govern', 'stars', 'life'. Similarly, two kinds of mood and tone are held in tension, not just by the different kinds of words she uses but their juxtaposition: the mood of vigour, action, effort, movement, energy: and the mood of stillness, silence, vastness

and immutability. Caught between the two, and created out
of the tension between the two, is a moment when the
turning-point between them is suggested as death and corruption. Energy and effort, everything that represents a certain
kind of indefatigable conscious human vitality of will, is im-
mutably and inexorably contained within a larger context in
which its only tenure is death.

In the pool which reflects the fixed stars, the rock thrown
with so much effort has become:

'A white skull,
Eaten by weedy greens'.

This poet, then, is communicating by a tension she perceives in the nature of words and their use, and by the way
she presents it, not merely the concrete and the particular in
the context of the eternal, but a profound sense of human
transience, isolation and corruption. By using the words she
does in the way she does, she has revealed a personal world
view to us. Denis Donoghue's comment on American poetic
usage is germane here, when (quoting Rosenberg and Roland
Barthes) he points out its disjunction, since it 'has no pre-
scribed relations' and is thereby 'so opposed to the social
function of language that merely to have recourse to (its)
discontinuous speech is to open the door to all that stands
above Nature. . . Modern language presupposes a discontinuous Nature.'[5]

There is one other thing we should note about the way
Sylvia Plath talks about words and their use. Her words make
an impact on us because she has contrived a context for them,
by means of the two images which control the whole poem.
That is, by using the axes and wood, and the rock and pool,
she has placed us, the hearers of her words, in a situation in
which we can do our own orienteering. Here she is following
a principle we would all recognise: that is, that words in use
must be located within a given situation which creates its own
understandable conventions and rules *to which those words*

must be true. Hence (a revealing example) part of the fascination of *Alice in Wonderland*: given each extraordinary situation there is a situational logic about the way words are used within that situation. The essential thing is to crack the code of the situation's linguistic convention.

Words in 'context'.

This brings us to the point where we can take the 'situational context' with words as objects or tools in it, as our next useful area of examination. Here it is valuable to start from the everyday and commonplace. A moment's thought will show us the relation of words to ordinary human living. Paul Van Buren summarised this very succinctly some years ago:

'Words – what are words? We all know perfectly well what they are, do we not? All we have to do is look (or listen) and see. And when we do, we see that in their natural habitat, words are found in the context of human life. Words are also found isolated from their natural habitat in spelling lists, grammar books, and dictionaries, which serve to teach the agreed use, spelling, and application of words, so that we can go out and use these words in action as others do. Normally, however, words are words-in-action and exist in the context of people doing things together.

People speak, usually to each other. Words are written and read, spoken and heard, in every connection and for every purpose which people make or have. Words used in series according to agreed patterns – language – are woven into the fabric of the whole complex of human life. Words are our tools for living. With words we build roads and houses and bridges. With words we encourage and discourage each other. Indeed, with these instruments we think and sing and tell stories and love and hate; in short, we live as human beings.

Words may be thought of also as acts. Much conversation, making of promises, writing poetry, and telling stories and jokes are occasions in which the speaking is the doing that we intend. Speaking is a distinctively human way of acting, and it is difficult to imagine human activity without its accompanying language. It is helpful, then, to think of language as behaviour, indeed, as distinctively human behaviour. It is our human way of going about all that we do.'[6]

Living as human beings, then, is reflected through words and the way we use them. A question about 'what a word means' includes questions about the person using it. It is true to say, therefore, that our living as human beings is in some sense defined by the way we use words. But we must go a little further than this since it is obvious that in some sense we are ourselves to some degree shaped by our use of words. This is not to suggest, at this point, that words (in the way we are speaking of them) are other than tools which take their life from their use: merely that the way the society, group, or others in a relationship uses them may finally help to shape what one is oneself. In extending one's own use of words, one is in fact to some degree shaping oneself (or being shaped, by the act of usage).

An excellent, even if hackneyed, example of both these aspects of the idea is to be found in Arnold Wesker's *Roots*, which was really all about this subject of the use of words in communication. The *credo* of his drama has consistently been that humanity finds fulfilment only when it finds articulacy, that the free and enjoyable handling of the language is essential to mature human beings, and that any social *mores* or structure which does not release this is crippling. (This chimes with the more systematic argument of, for instance, the '*nouvelle critique*', whose view of the writer's actualising of his perceptions is that it is discovered in the process of handling of the language:

> 'The artist does not first intuit his object and then find the appropriate medium. It is rather in and through his medium that he intuits.'[7])

Mr. Polly, in H. G. Well's book of that name, is a rather pleasant fictional representative of the same view. He trium-

phantly escapes from the pressure of his society's *mores*, showing the first signs of doing this in his loving and highly
idiosyncratic misuse of words whose meaning is unknown to
him but whose sound he likes. Similarly, by the end of Wesker's play, *Roots*, Beatie, the inarticulate heroine, though she
has lost her lover, has learnt to use words for herself and not
merely echo what her lover has said. She joyfully proclaims:

'I'm talking – listen to me someone – I'm not quoting no more!'

and the curtain falls on her articulacy. There is a famous
passage in the play when all this is explicitly expressed:

'Beatie: . . . There was a time when he handled all official
things for me, you know. Once I was in between jobs
and I didn't think to ask for my unemployment
benefit. He told me to. But when I asked they told me
I was short on stamps and so I wasn't entitled to
benefit. I didn't know what to say but he did. He went
up and argued for me – he's just like his mother, she
argues with everyone – and I got it. I didn't know how
to talk see, it was all foreign to me. Think of it! An
English girl born and bred and I couldn't talk the
language – except for to buy food and clothes. And so
sometimes when he were in a black mood he'd start on
me. "What can you talk of?", he'd ask. "Go on, pick a
subject. Talk. Use the language. Do you know what
language is?" Well, I'd never thought before – hev
you? – it's automatic to you, isn't it, like walking?
"Well, language is words", he'd say, as though he were
telling me a secret. "It's bridges, so that you can get
safely from one place to another. And the more bridges
you know about the more places you can see!. . ." '[8]

We might note that Doris Lessing, much more recently
and in an entirely different context, made her perceptive
heroine, a 'guardian' of the good, comment similarly:

'In this effort of speech was the energy of frustration: this

31

child, like others formed by our old time which above all had been verbal, to do with words, the exchange of them, the use of them, had been excluded from all that richness. We (meaning the educated) had never found a way of sharing that plenty with the lower reaches of our society. Even in two women standing on a street's edge bartering their few sentences of gossip had been the explosive effort of frustration: the deprived, thinned speech of the poor had always had somewhere in it the energy of a resentment (unconscious perhaps, but there) fed by the knowledge of skills and ease just beyond them, and whose place in their talk was taken by the constant repetition of the phrases – like crutches – "you know?" and "you know what I mean?" and "isn't it?" and all the rest, phrases which made up a good part of everything they said. Words in their mouths . . . had a labouring, effortful quality – dreadful, because of the fluencies so easily available, but to others.'[9]

'Effecting' words.

Aside from the (very important) social implications of such passages, which we shall look at in more detail in chapter four, there is a more basic concept of word-use arising in these passages. Words in the communication process are used, first, *to get things done*, actions initiated, points made clear, in the ordinary twentieth-century world of income tax and allow- ances, bureaucracy and social welfare services, shopping and dressing: and secondly, to develop, slowly and carefully, a wider vision of life, and of relationships to the point where they are loving. Both uses are of a positive nature, both are essential to the human organisation, societally and familially, but they exist at very different levels. One is the public use of words, the other the private use, and to this distinction between the public and the private voice we shall return later. The definition we must concentrate on, first, is the 'income tax' one, primarily concerned with defining, clarifying, the making of as accurate a statement of the situation as can be rationally and logically conceived. The other is directed to- wards not simply the clarification of but the development of something – in this case a relationship – even to the point where something new has been created.

To take the first. Here the use of words has as its matrix that which is rational and logical. It is directed towards a situation which is to be supposed intelligible, within a universe which is orderly and coherent. Now, if we relate this back to that idea of the world in flux, which in John Osborne's expression we noted at the beginning of this chapter, we begin to see that two views of word-use are set on collision course. The philosophy behind the pragmatic 'dailiness' of word-use, that is, is opposed by implication to the linguistic anarchy of much current thought.

C. B. Cox, as long ago as 1972, sounded in *The Critical Quarterly* the warning note about a philosophy of word-use which rejected the intelligible:

> 'These views . . . . are often implicit in neo-modernistic forms in art, and in much of the dominating "pop" culture. "Order" is rejected as part of an adolescent metaphysical view of the world, and with this rejection goes the traditional Apollonian notion of the artist as someone who imposes form and order on life, on the raw flux of experience. Instead there is a preference for the random, the inconsequential, for anti-art. Such views can only regard university literary studies with contempt, for these depend on belief in the value of the controlling, ordering, rational intellect. I have yet to hear (though I expect to do so any day) of a university lecturer who has suggested to his students that their essays would be improved if each page had a hole in it so we could see, in random fashion, the pages beneath.'[10]

Though this attack seems now in some ways curiously dated, there is an important sense in which the battle is still being waged with heat. For the struggle is, if anything, heightened, currently, to establish a controlling ideology for writing and reading. The ideology implied by the 'random' denies not only Cox's traditional 'Apollonian notion of the artist as someone who imposes form and order on life', but also denies that understanding of words which relates them to orderly principles in the universe; a concept which was, incidentally, a common meeting ground between Christian and non-Christian.

The word of power.

The other main aspect of the everyday use of words in communication, apart from that of getting things done in an intelligible society, was, as illustrated from the passage in *Roots*, the use of language to explore and create relationships.

> 'No bridges, I'd say – and we'd row. Sometimes he hurt me, but then, slowly, he'd build the bridge up for me – and then we'd make love!'[11]

Here we make a very important shift between two quite different kinds of concept of 'word'. We are beginning to move from 'word' as a mere tool, taking its vitality from its use in a given situation, to something which perhaps has more power: we are, that is, beginning to move through the concepts of word as 'disclosure', and word as 'an act', till we reach, compassing the two, word as 'event'. At the point at which it becomes an 'event' we are reaching a much more controversial and less definable area. Yet it is one which every creative writer, every sensitive reader, and every theologian, is aware of and is challenged to engage at some point. It is, of course, the 'word of power'. It is more than time, critically, to re-emphasise this 'dynamos', this word of power, this 'seizing' of the artist. Current literary debate has moved so far in the direction of 'reader power' (to quote Caroline Belsey[12]) that the activity of the artist other than as a theoretical, necessary, but non-defining source of the words on the page has not only lost primacy, but even *recognition*, as of 'power', in any sense. The strange and arbitrary nature of the 'imagination' has been cast aside by linguistic rationalism or nihilism.

We may therefore, profitably, approach this first from the writer's point of view. Charlotte Bronte, in defending her sister Emily's book, *Wuthering Heights*, in the preface to the second edition, spoke of the moment which comes to each writer when the creation he is at work on suddenly takes on its own life, obeys its own laws, and while it is in some sense subject to his shaping, yet retains its own integrity and power:

'The writer who possesses the creative gift owns something of which he is not always master – something that at times strangely wills and works for itself. He may lay down rules and devise principles, and to rules and principles it will perhaps for years lie in subjection; and then, haply without any warning of revolt, there comes a time when it will no longer consent. . . When, refusing absolutely to make ropes out of seasand any longer, it sets to work on statue-hewing, and you have a Pluto or a Jove. . . . as Fate or Inspiration direct. Be the work grim or glorious, dread or divine, you have little choice left but quiescent adoption. As for you – the nominal artist – your share in it has been to work passively under dictates you neither delivered nor could question.'[13]

One hundred and twenty years later Harold Pinter expressed this same experience. In his plays he is clearly fascinated by the problem of communicating the incommunicable and by the fastidiously exact phrase by which the truth must be sifted. When receiving the Shakespeare Prize in Hamburg in 1970, he said:

'I believe myself that when a writer looks at the blank of the word he has not yet written, or when actors and directors arrive at a given moment on stage, there is only one proper thing that can take place at that moment, and that that thing, that gesture, that word on the page, must alone be found, and once found, scrupulously protected. I think I am talking about necessary shape, both as regards a play and its production.

If there is, as I believe, a necessary, an obligatory shape which a play demands of its writer, then I have never been able to achieve it myself. I have always finished the last draft of a play with a mixture of feelings: relief, disbelief, exhilaration, and a certainty that if I could only wring the play's neck once more it might yield once more to me, that I could get it better, that I could get the better of it, perhaps. But that's impossible. You create the word and in a certain way the word, in finding its own life, stares you out, is obdurate, and more often than not defeats you. . . . And there's a third and rarer pain. That is when the right word, or the right act jolts (the characters) or stills them into their proper life. When that happens the pain is worth having.'

In his view, therefore, necessity and propriety somehow come together so that the word is 'finding its own life'.

'I am aware, sometimes of an insistence in my mind. Images, characters, insisting upon being written. You can pour a drink, make a telephone call or run round the park, and sometimes succeed in suffocating them. You know they're going to make your life hell. But at other times they're unavoidable and you're compelled to try to do them some kind of justice. And while it may be hell, it's certainly for me the best kind of hell to be in.'

Here words are still functioning as *words in use*: but they are being treated somehow differently, with the sort of respect we give to that which is self-authenticating. It is this kind of use of words we now need to look at more fully. Again, we may usefully do so by means of a twentieth century literary expression of it.

Word as 'event'.

There is a passage in John Osborne's *Luther*, which fascinatingly explores the many sides of this self-authentication of some words in use. Osborne was interested in Luther as a man of the Word (with an upper-case 'W') and it is the paradox inherent in this which he is expressing dramatically. There is, first the Knight's speech placed in the play long after the Diet of Worms, spoken looking down at the corpse of a peasant killed in the Peasants' Revolt:

'Knight: There was excitement that day. In Worms – that day
I mean. . . I tell you, you can't have ever known the
kind of thrill that monk set off amongst that collection
of all kinds of men gathered together there – those
few years ago. We all felt it, every one of us, just
without any exception, you couldn't help it, even if
you didn't want to. . . . But he fizzed like a hot spark
in a trail of gunpowder going off in us, that dowdy
monk, he went off in us, and nothing could stop it,
and it blew up and there was nothing we could do,
any of us, that was it. . . . I just felt quite sure, quite
certain in my own mind nothing could ever be the
same again, just simply that. Something had taken
place, something had changed and become something
else, an event had occurred in the flesh, in the flesh
and the breath – like, even like when the weight of
that body slumped on its wooden crotchpiece and the
earth grew dark. That's the kind of thing I mean by
happen, and this also happened in very likely the
same manner to all those of us who stood there,
friends and enemies alike.'[14]

Two ideas, of word as 'revelation' and word as 'creative
act', are brought together here to form a third word, word as
'event'. Certain implied qualities of this demand our attention.
(We should remember that this is the writer who spoke of the
'old bardic belief' in words.)

First of all, we should note that 'word in use' here is the
'corporate' word: it is addressed to a collection of men of all
kinds, and sympathy towards it is not a necessary factor: 'you
couldn't help it, even if you didn't want to'. Yet it has individual validity also – 'every *one* of us', the Knight says, 'felt
it', and he goes on, 'I just felt quite sure, quite certain in my
own mind. . . .' Corporate, yet individual; and in both cases
almost irresistible: this is the first quality adduced in word as
event.

The second is that which really defines it. The revelation
which is given through *this* kind of word being spoken is some

kind of disclosure through which something is changed and become something else. So the speaking of the word becomes a 'happening', with the kind of vital quality which not only changes things and people but recreates them. This kind of use of word, which has such power that it results in the change of the old order of things and a new order created, occurs within the context of the concrete and particular which yet is given a cosmological and even sacred extension. There is emphasis on time, place, person – '*that* day' – in 'Worms' – *that* dowdy monk'. But the words in use, 'that day', 'in Worms', 'by that dowdy monk', are set in the context of an event in the 'flesh' – all flesh – and the 'breath', and finally in the context of the Crucifixion itself which is seen as of cosmic significance, 'as the earth grew dark'. So words as 'events' in this particular play take their nature directly, are rooted in, whatever the nature of the 'event' of the Cross.

There is one other point we should note about Osborne's suggestion of the power of word as event. That is, that it is conceived in the context of a trial. Law, judgment and proclamation are all aspects of this word which exploded like a hot spark in a trail of gunpowder. Words in the communication process, at whatever level in defining or exploring must assess, must judge.[15] Always they have to be discriminating. When they are set in the context of ultimate faith and ultimate judgment, or personal belief and cosmic significance, then the 'law' to which they have reference is extended indefinitely and becomes 'Law'.

This leads us in the play to the encounter between the Knight and Luther in which the Knight asserts that all the political upheavals of the land have arisen from the 'word as event' earlier described; and he challenges Luther because of it. There follows a fascinating dramatic confrontation over what has been the true quality of word as event: what are, and must be recognised to be, its limitations; or its infinities:

'Knight: Don't hold your Bible to my head, piggy, there's
enough revelation of my own in there for me, in what

              I see for myself from here! (Taps his forehead.) Hold
              your gospel against that!
(The Knight grabs Martin's hand and clamps it to his
head.). . . .

Knight: You're killing the spirit, and you're killing it with the
        letter. You've been swilling about in the wrong place,
        Martin, in your own stink and ordure. Go on! You've
        got your hand on it, that's all the holy spirit there is,
        and it's all you'll ever get, so feel it!

        (They struggle, but the Knight is very weak by now,
        and Martin, is able to wrench himself away and up
        into the pulpit.)

Martin: The word was conquered by the Word, the Church is
        maintained by the Word –

Knight: Word? What Word? Word? That word, whatever that
        means, is probably just another old relic or indulgence,
        and you know what you did to those! Why, none of it
        might be any more than poetry, have you thought of
        that, Martin? Poetry! Martin, you're a poet, there's no
        doubt about that in anybody's mind, you're a poet,
        but do you know what most men believe in, in their
        hearts – because they don't see in images like you do –
        they believe in their hearts that Christ was a man as
        we are, and that he was a prophet and a teacher, and
        they also believe in their hearts that his supper is a
        plain meal like their own – if they're lucky enough to
        get it – a plain meal of bread and wine! A plain meal
        with no garnish and no word. And *you* helped them to
        begin to believe it!

Martin: (pause) Leave me.

Knight: Yes. What's there to stay for? I've been close enough
        to you for too long. I even smell like you.

Martin: (roaring with pain) I smell because of my own
        argument, I smell because I never stop disputing with
        him, and because I expect him to keep his Word. Now
        then! If your peasant rebelled against that Word, that

was worse than murder because it laid the whole
country waste, and who knows now what God will
make of us Germans!'[16]

The Knight's assertions about 'Word' are, therefore, that all
revelation can only be of men, for there is nothing other to
know. When Martin's hand is on his head, for the Knight at
that moment, he says, Martin's hand is spanning the only
'holy spirit' there is.

The 'Word' and word

In this verbal struggle the really crucial question about the
use of words in communication is pushed straight before us.
The Knight speaks of the 'word', a word without power, a
word which is a tool for use only, like a plain meal of bread
and wine with no garnish. That is what he has understood
the 'word as event' in Worms to mean. Luther is pressing
home a profoundly different meaning of Word, that of the
power of God in action on earth. The one is talking about the
language by which man defines himself; the other is talking
about the means of God's self-disclosure. Ultimately, one's
view of the communication possible through words derives
from which understanding one has of the word as event. What
lies behind the anger of the Knight (and in his voice we hear
what is today a widely and consistently held critical view) is
that the word as revelation, as self-disclosure, must be fo-
cussed only on what men can wholly agree on as possible
referents. It is defined by the material universe: a plain meal
of bread, wine, no garnish and no extraterrestrial word.

What of the understanding that Luther has? He is presented
as a man roaring with pain, because he is caught in the eternal
dispute which every prophet and every artist has suffered,
between his 'God's' self-disclosure and his own dispute with
him. 'I expect him to keep his Word', he says; that is, words
as self-disclosure must carry the integrity of the Being dis-
closed. Van Buren, it will be remembered, pointed out that
one cannot talk about the meaning of words without talking

about the person using them. The Word referred to in Luther's speech is the word of authority; that aspect of the nature of God which Martin expects God to be true to and vindicate and which gives him the security and freedom of dispute in the human currency of words. The agony in the dispute arises, as for the prophets it has so often arisen, from the apparent lack of vindication of that very quality to whose existence Martin is committed.

There is another point connected with the word as event which we should notice. We have just seen that Martin is roaring with pain, that he is repellent and unlovely, rejected by his fellows. In the first part of the Knight's musing about the word, the image of word as event was of gunpowder and destruction: the emphasis was on something explosive and destroying. If something became something else it was because of an experience described in terms of destruction, the death-slump, and universal darkness.

So the words used to communicate truth of a universal kind must have a matrix adequate to the whole of reality. Any ideology, therefore, in which word-use is to be critically grounded needs to be formulated in such terms as compass, adequately, known forces of destruction as well as known good, dereliction as well as joy. Later we shall look more closely at what this implies theologically. The use of words to explore and define the nature of suffering, death and evil demands criticism whose context is an adequate theology of creation, judgment and salvation. An 'ideology' of criticism which does not supply these is inadequate to the art it purposes to debate.

Yet if the extraordinary power that word as event has can be related to the fullness of the incarnate Word of God, as Christians would assert, then words in use in communication must be true to all the aspects of that power. They must carry within the context of 'judgment' and 'authority' that self-authenticating revelation which speaks and changes. This must remain true in the words used in our twentieth century, with its fragmented consciousness, escapist fantasy, and search for experience for its own sake; and herein lies a problem, since such words must also be true to their cultural and temporal context. Prophetic utterance, words-in-use for the communication of creative authority, judging, and healing, are as relevant today as ever but their idiom is less accessible.[17] Indeed, some 'structuralists' would argue that the very concepts are irrelevant since language use relates to no final reality. (We shall look at this more closely in chapter four.)

'Public' and 'private' language

We noticed earlier, very briefly, the distinction between the 'public' and 'private' use of words. Prophetic utterance is 'public'; but since today we are islanded in our linguistic anarchy or impoverishment, each man has, perhaps more than ever before, a private language. An attempt to meet this in literary terms is to be found in Edward Albee's *Who's afraid of Virginia Woolf?*. The dramatist broke through the problem by deliberately intertwining the two languages, creating a dramatic situation in which the conventions allow for both. (We noticed before how words must operate within the conventions of the situation obtaining.) The dramatic situation is the death of the child of the house. The language which is private, which is between husband and wife and their visitors, about the news of the death and the reaction to it, is balanced by the language which is public, the Latin recital of parts of the Mass for the Burial of the Dead. Component elements of it are the *Kyrie*, *Dies Irae*, the Absolution, the *Pax*, and the *Lux Perpetua*.

But the use of the two kinds of words is much more subtle than that. The husband and wife are also George and Martha, representative middle-aged Americans: and the child who is dead never existed; he is a dream son who has lived only in their fantasy world. He is the American dream of the perfect society built up on a perfect generation, with sun-blond hair, leading his elders into the fields of Paradise. So the private language has societal reference: public connotation. Similarly the public language, that of the Mass for the Dead, has private connotation. Martha in particular is haunted, even possessed by, this fantasy child: and so the incantation is an exorcism of her haunted spirit:[8]

'George: Our child.

Martha: Our child. And we raised him. . . . Yes we did; we raised him. . . .
And his eyes were green. . . . green with. . . . if you peered so deep into them. . . . so deep . . . .
bronze. . . . bronze parentheses around the irises. . . . such green eyes!

George: . . . . blue, green, brown. . . .

Martha: . . . and he loved the sun!. . . . He was tan before and after everyone. . . . and in the sun his hair. . . . became fleece.

George: . . . . fleece . . . .

Martha: . . . . beautiful, beautiful boy.

George: Absolve, Domine, animas omnium fidelium defunctorum ab omni vinculo delictorum.

Martha: . . . . and school . . . . and summer camp. . . . and sledding. . . . and swimming. . . . .

George: Et gratia tua illis succurrente, mereantur avadere judicium ultionis.

Martha: . . . . and how he broke his arm. . . . how funny it was. . . . oh, no, it hurt him!. . . . but oh, it was funny. . . . in a field, his very first cow, the first he'd ever seen. . . . and he went into the field, to the cow, where the cow was grazing, head down, busy. . . . and he moo'd at it!. . . . and the beast, oh, surprised, swung its head up and moo'd at him, all three years of him, and he ran, startled, and he stumbled. . . . fell. . . . and broke his poor arm. Poor lamb.

George: Et lucis aeternae beatitudine perfrui.

Martha: George cried! Helpless. . . . George. . . . cried. I

carried the poor lamb. George snuffling beside me, I
carried the child, having fashioned a sling. . . . and
across the great fields.

George: In Paradisum deducant te Angeli.

Martha: And as he grew. . . . and as he grew. . . . oh! so wise!
He walked evenly between us. . . . a hand out to each
of us for what we could offer by way of support
affection, teaching, even love. . . . and these hands,
still, to hold us off a bit for mutual protection, to
protect us all from George's . . . . weakness. . . . and
my necessary greater strength. . . . to protect
himself. . . . and us.

George: In memoria aeterna erit justus: ab auditione mala non
timebit. . . . .

. . . .Martha: Of course, this state, this perfection. . . .
couldn't last. Not with George. . . . not with
George around.

(BOTH TOGETHER)

Martha: I have tried, oh
God I have tried;
the one thing. . . .
the one thing I've
tried to carry pure
and   unscathed
through the sewer
of this marriage;
through the sick
nights, and the pa-
thetic, stupid days,
through the deri-
sion and the laugh-
ter. . . . God, the
laughter, through
one failure after an-
other, one failure
compounding an-

George: Libera me, Dom-
ine, de morte ae-
terna, in die illa
tremenda: Quando
caeli movendi sunt
et terra: Dum ve-
neris judicare sacu-
ulum per ignem.
Tremens   factus
sum ego, et timeo,
dum discussio ve-
nerit, atque ventura
ira. Quando caeli
movendi sunt et
terra. Dies illa, dies
erae, calamitatis et
miseriae,   dies
magna at amara

other failure, each attempt more sickening, more numbing than the one before; the one thing, the one person I have tried to protect, to raise above the mire of this vile, crushing marriage; the one light in all this hopeless . . . darkness . . . OUR SON.

valde. Dum veneris judicare saecumum per ignem. Requiem aeternam dona eis, Domine; et lux perpetua luceat eis. Libera me Domine de morte aeterna in die illa tremenda: Quando caeli movendi sunt et terra: Dum veneris judicare saeculum per ignem.

(END TOGETHER)

Honey: STOP IT!! STOP IT!!
George: Kyrie, eleison. Christe, eleison. Kyrie eleison.'

The two languages not only twine together, but even, as above, are spoken simultaneously, to emphasise their mutual relevance. The 'event' which takes place is that Martha is 'exorcised' and from that exorcism their two young visitors (who are also their successors in the public, corporate life) depart having shared the private experience, wanting, for the first time, to have a child: new life is possible out of the 'wholeness' of utterance.

In sum, then, it will be apparent that in looking at the way modern artists are thinking about and handling words we begin to see, in words as 'tools', as 'contextured', and 'effective', but above all in the dynamic concept of word as event, with its fusion of the public and private, and its element of 'judgment', glimpses of a discernible pattern of word-use, some of which at least can be assimilated to a Christian understanding of God as Creator and particularly to the Logos creation. We shall look at this in much more detail in the next chapter.

45

CHAPTER THREE

A model of making

'I believe in God, Maker. . . .'[1]

We come now to a consideration of some of the implications theologically of that credal statement; and to the 'model' of 'divine making' that it generates. From there we shall move to a possible theological formulation of human making (one of many ?), and finally to one or two critical inferences that are possible.

In the beginning: eternal energy and historic figure.

'I believe in God, Maker. . . .' With a certain obviousness we must start by noting that the doctrinal continuity of Old and New Testaments is affirmed by the style of their opening words. The Book of Genesis goes back to the first conceivable action: 'In the beginning God created'. The Gospel of John goes behind even this, to the first conceivable creative existence: 'In the beginning was the Word and the Word was with God and the Word was God'. Through the Word 'all things were made' and without him 'was not anything made that was made'. The Word is immediately identified, therefore, in two different ways. First, with the origin of life, vitality: 'In him was life' (or, as the marginal reading puts it, 'That which has been made was life in him'). Second: with the historical/eternal figure of Jesus Christ: 'And the Word became flesh and dwelt among us, full of grace and truth.'

This link, between God, life and Jesus Christ, is repeatedly made explicit in the Gospel of John, by symbolic narrative, by discourse, by images and by summary. Not the least crucial and enigmatic summary of the relationship occurs in John chapter five, 'For as the Father has life in himself, so he has granted the Son to have life in himself'. Inherent life, life 'in himself' or 'of himself', is seen as a quality pertaining to that Creative Being who is God, different in some way from that which other beings enjoy, but shared by the historical figure, Jesus Christ, 'the Word'. We shall return to this later, but we might note in passing how it links with what writers have recorded of their own experience.[2]

The role of Christ in God's making and re-making.

This quality of 'inherent life' in God the Creator, life of which Jesus Christ is the agent, is hymned as early as the record of 1 Corinthians:

> 'Yet for us there is one God, the Father, from whom are all things and for whom we exist, and one Lord, Jesus Christ, through whom are all things and through whom we exist.'

The use of the prepositions is, of course, critical here. God is that life which is our source and end: Jesus is the Mediator through whom that life is realised and sustained. The life is *both* that life seen as everywhere expressed by the whole order of creation: *and also* that new life mediated by Jesus in the new orientation to God of his redeemed creatures.[3]

Christ *both* saves *and* creates: the 'dia' prepositions – 'through our Lord Jesus Christ' – realise and celebrate the function of Christ in creation simultaneously with his agency in salvation: they remind us that inherent in his power are both redemptive and creative qualities. His power in creation and salvation is at once extra-temporal – outside time; particular – located in time; immediate – of direct force and effect; and ongoing – not concluded by the immediate occasion of its operation, but continuing for ever.[4]

It is these aspects of Christ's role in God's making and re-making of his creation which are referred to in 2 Corinthians:

'Therefore, if anyone is in Christ, he is a new creation. The old has passed away, behold, the new has come. All this is from God, who through Christ reconciled us to himself and gave us the ministry of reconciliation.'[5]

In looking at the relationship between God's 'making' and man's, therefore, we cannot too early identify the continuity of God's acts in creation with God's acts in redemption: Christ being both the means of and incarnate extension of those acts. For this has important implications for our understanding of man the maker: it helps us to see him as sharing a saving role. If his creative making is truly grounded in a theology of God the Creator, not only is its final role one of affirmation, but when man most truly 'makes' it is for the healing of nations. For there is no final discontinuity or disjunction in the rela-tionship of God the Creator to his creation: that which he created he redeems and as he redeems so he re-creates:[6]

'In many and various ways God spoke of old to our fathers by the prophets: but in these last days he has spoken to us by a Son, whom he appointed the heir of all things, through whom also he created the world. He reflects the glory of God and bears the very stamp of his nature, upholding the universe by his word of power.'[7]

This enlargement in the Epistle to the Hebrews of the creation/salvation statements about God emphasises three things particularly. The first, as we have just noted, in the continuousness of God's living relationship with his creation. The second is that the Son, Jesus Christ, through whom the world was created, in some sense reflects the 'glory' of God. The third is that 'power' is involved, such power as upholds the universe; and that this power is expressed through 'word', which immediately refers us back to the beginning of the passage, to the variety of 'word' God has used in communication to his people, and also to the variety of word the 'fathers' and the 'prophets' have used to express to their generations God's message. Within our present argument it also refers us to our earlier discussion of word as 'power'.[8]

I shall return to the concept of glory in making later, merely noting that it is emphasised here in the context of Christ's role as himself the 'message' of God and as agent and sustainer of creation. Christ is, so to speak, an act of glory. This suggests something about the nature of creation itself, and its ongoing life. It suggests, as Browning would say, a tremor of joy, a 'blink of glory', in created life itself.

The continuousness of creation.

And secondly, this concept of 'glory' glows throughout that very continuity of God's creative relationship with what he has made, that faithfulness, which we have already noticed. As we saw, in what are thought to be amongst the earliest Christian confessions this creative constancy is asserted. It is not merely that it was a logical step for the young Church to see in the agent of the new Creation the one through whom creation first came to be. Rather, as Gustav Aulen has pointed out:

'The act of creation loses its meaning. . . . if it is reduced to only an initial action performed once in the past, if creation were something that has stopped, if it were not an action of God constantly going on anew.'[9]

God is the one 'who acts', and the he 'who was, is and shall be'; and so creation is in a real sense a continuous enactment, the dynamic force which makes the God/man relationship unchanging and secure; that which both prevents it from becoming static and yet provides for God's 'trust-worthiness'. Peter Smulders insists on the same idea, pointing out that in both Deutero-Isaiah in the Old Testament and in the Gospels, Epistles and Apocalypse we have the idea of God's creative activity, *not* as the setting up of a stable cosmic order, once for all time, but a state of continuous 'happening'. He too suggests that 'creating' and 'redeeming' are almost the same act, pointing out that this is certainly the case in Isaiah.[10] Creation is an act of the present instant: the whole reality of the world, not just its beginning but its whole existence including its consummation.[11] Moreover, this creative activity was seen as spontaneous, having no other cause or sense but the initiative of love. It was not, that is, that God is to be understood as having 'made something' and then wondered what to do with it: rather, that it follows from the engagement of the Creator with his creation that from the first the creative purpose was one of profound and secure relationship, to be felicitious and glorious. (I shall say more of this later.)

This brings us to the third element in the introduction quoted from the Epistle to the Hebrews, that of 'word'. We have already spent some time on this in chapter two, and now need to look more closely at the biblical theology of it. Whether it is the word of law spoken by God to the 'fathers' of Israel and to the prophets, and through them to his people, or whether it is the word spoken by God through Christ to create and sustain the universe extra-temporally on the one hand, and historically to preach the Kingdom of God on the other: it is a word of 'power'. Different though it is in so many ways from the other Epistles and from the Gospels, the Epistle to the Hebrews significantly meshes closely with what they have to say in using the concept 'word of power' to explore God's creative/redemptive act.

Aspects of 'Logos'.

It is therefore to the special use of 'word', 'Logos' in the New Testament, we turn now. Of the complex range of ideas associated with it I want to touch, and then only briefly, on three. One is the Greek-Hebrew tension in the use of the concept. Second, following from this, is its enrichment by the Hebraic pattern of thought about the role of 'Wisdom' in creation; and a third is the sense in which we may identify 'Logos' with Christ the Word.

50

Most of us are familiar with the Greek understanding of 'Logos' which was in no sense a word of creative power: thus, as has been expounded elsewhere in detail, its usage stands in contrast with the 'word' of the Hebrews.[12] It always referred to something natural 'even to the extent that the account of a thing and the thing itself merge so that "Logos" is to be translated "thing" '.[13] Or it was a 'reckoning' in the sense of a principle of law discoverable through calculation, or reason, the product of thought and calculation. It could be the enumeration in the correct order of the elements in a subject. Or, more profoundly, it was the establishment of the particular; the definition, sometimes even the nature or essence. Logos could, therefore, be a 'significant utterance'. The important element in the Greek usage for us, therefore, in this discussion is the dianoetic value of 'Logos'. That is, that it contains a *nous*, thought, by which a thing is known and grasped. To grasp the Logos in this sense is to grasp the thing itself – i.e. its nature is brought to light.

But there is no sense in which this is revelation from God to man. Rather it is:

'Revelation only in the sense that one perceives the inner law of the matter, or of self, and orientates oneself thereby.'[14]

By contrast the Hebraic use of the verbal equivalent predominant in New Testament usage, even in John, was revelatory and dynamic. Knecht writes:

'Only in the Hebrew is the material concept with its energy felt so vitally in the verbal concept that the word appears as a material force which is always present and at work, which runs and has the power to make alive.'[15]

Thus it is that the prophets, for instance, are seized by God, by his spirit and his word: the power of God finds recognisable expression in that *Logos* which is law, which is prophecy, and which is often accompanied by signs and images. Indeed, it was the experience of this 'seizing' by a power felt to be benign, and understood initially in terms of God's loving care for his people, which led to a belief in the whole creation as an extension of faith in the Lord, God of the Covenant. Thus it is, too, that another sphere of revelation, Nature, has everywhere in the Old Testament its creation attributed to the word of God, owing its extension to God's address to it. Genesis chapter one embodies this, and may itself be a re-fashioning of an older account, the work God does (chapter two, verse two) being replaced by the word he speaks.[16]

It is the coming together of both the Hellenic and Hebraic understandings of word that makes the 'Logos' usage in the New Testament so richly germane to our thinking.[17] The word is a message that corresponds to a reality: and that reality corresponded precisely with the historical figure the apostolic age had known:

'That which was from the beginning, which we have heard, which we have seen with our eyes, which we have looked upon and touched with our hands, concerning the word of life – the life was made manifest, and we saw it, and testify to it. . . . . and we are writing this that our (your?) joy may be complete.'[18]

Hence there is in the figure of Christ as 'Word' both the Hellenic suggestion that by this there can be revelation of a self-authenticating kind, reality can be known and grasped, 'the account of a thing and the thing itself merge' in a way and in a sense not guessed at by the Greeks, and yet there is the dynamic and revelatory 'seizing', creative prompting and initiating, which is wholly Hebraic. Alasdair Heron has noted that it was this inter-connectedness which the Apologists took over in order to articulate their Logos christology, one which served a function till Nicea completed the change of model by affirming the primary paradigm of 'Jesus, the Son of God'. But before that could happen, the Logos image was required to supply 'a way of understanding what it meant to talk of a "Son of God" at all':

'The connection of the Logos with rationality and revelation on the one hand and with creation and cosmogony on the other, a connection which the Apologists took over from earlier theories of the Logos, was an essential pre-supposition for the articulation of their Logos christology.'[19]

It is not only, however, that to look at the Logos concept is to expose some of the history lying behind our current credal formulation. It is that when we are thinking about what we mean by the act of God (through Christ) in creation, or the act of God (through Christ) in salvation – what did God actually 'do' in these acts of making and re-making? – we find the others have earlier used the phrase 'word of power' to describe the 'doing'. And that when they spoke of the Logos – the word of power of God – behind their phrase there lay the idea of both rationality, order, coherence, an orderliness affirmed in the person of Christ who himself embodies it; and yet also within the phrase vibrates the idea of energy 'which runs and has the power to make alive', which materialises itself, which seizes the person and breaks through the formula, which regenerates and transforms. Behind this vitality lies that part of the 'Wisdom' pattern of creation which lays emphasis on the *paradoxical* nature of the activity of God.

One aspect of this paradoxical activity has to do with the tension between the secret and hidden nature of God's 'Wisdom' in making (1 Corinthians 1.20, 2.16: cf. with The Wisdom of Solomon 13.1–9), as opposed to the 'public' foolishness of human wisdom. This 'secret and hidden' Wisdom of the creation is also to be found in God's 're-making' on the Cross and in God's decree, before the ages, of our own glorification.[20] Barbour relates this tension between Wisdom and foolishness to the *continuity* between the Old and New Testaments – it is the work of Wisdom to re-assert the original purpose and restore the distorted – on the one hand, and the *unforeseen*, the unexpected and wholly new, work of God's redemption on the other:

> 'That men should die and be resurrected was not wholly unexpected in Judaism; that God himself should in some sense do so was totally unexpected and there is nothing in the order of creation that points towards it.'[21]

This leads us to a second enrichment of the Logos creation tradition through Wisdom material, one which links also with the Apologists referred to earlier. For both in their writing and in the working out of the Wisdom material an inevitable difficulty arises; how can Christ be both Creator and created?

> 'As soon as we say that wisdom became man, or that the Logos became flesh, we introduce a conceptual distinction between that Wisdom that was in the beginning and ever shall be, and the human existence which was also "Wisdom" but was not in the beginning.'[22]

The christological consequences of this difficulty are considerable, and we shall look very briefly at some of them later, in the concluding chapter. In the meantime, the suggestion Professor Barbour makes to meet the difficulty has not only general but particular consequence for us in the local context in which we look at the problem:

> 'Perhaps the pondering of a paradox will help us a little: only the Creator can create his own creativeness, and only he who has done this can be seen at the deepest to be the Creator; *for the only truly creative and sovereign act visible to man is the act of self-abnegation in love* – nothing else represents unconquerable power.'[23]

I would add the proviso that 'self-abnegation' should bear a gloss which directs its intent to a glad self-emptying as a positive and loving act. Such, surely, lies behind the New Testament assertion that it is through Christ exalted and crucified that all things were made.

'Logos' as 'event'.

This fusion of the rational Hellenic with all the paradoxical energy that went to make up the Hebraic, leads us on to see the Logos-Christ figure as paradigmatic for creation as 'event', the category we have already recognised as attaching to certain kinds of human 'making' with words.[24] It is essential that we apprehend this fusion. To disregard it is to fall into the sort of theological narrowness exemplified by, for instance, Philip Wheelwright's exegesis, in his study in *Religion and Poetry* of John's description of Jesus as 'the Word': his (critically correct) view is that it:

> '. . . . represents a double semantic shift. There is a synecdochic shift from the whole to the part, whereby the writer, in order to speak about the Supreme Reality, concentrates on one attribute at a time. And there is the metaphoric shift from abstract to concrete, whereby the attribute thus momentarily isolated is presented under the figure of a familiar image.'[25]

This is a good example of meticulous literary criticism not fully grounded in the theology of the issue, since its emphasis is almost wholly on the Hellenic understanding of 'Word'. If we place it alongside Kittel's comment on the same topic, we note the contrast:

> 'At the head of the train of thought sketched by the term "Logos" there stands, not a concept, but the event which has taken place and in which God declares himself, causing his Word to be enacted. . . . .

> It is wrong to speak of a personification of the Logos in John 1.1, 14. This idea arises exclusively under the influence of non-biblical rather than biblical thought. It is possible only where there is something to be personified, i.e. something which may be abstracted from the person and envisaged as an idea outside it. New Testament thinking. . . . . has no primary interest in a world of reason of a semi-divine intermediate being, the Logos, which it is essential to describe and which, among other things, entered one day into the person of an earthly man. . . . It has no interest in ideas, not even in theological ideas. Its sole concern is with what has taken place in the person of Jesus. This event is set in its eternal framework.'[26]

Christ the Word, therefore, is not an unmaterialised concept.

He is an event, a revelation of God, assessable only in its own terms, owning its own vitality and life. Nor is any distinction to be drawn in this 'event' between his speech, his action and his being. They are a unity: three aspects of the *same event*, and to be experienced as such, so extended that ultimately Logos comes to contain the whole range of the Christian message.[27]

Kittel argues:

'There are not two Words of God but only one, which is given as such in the continuity and unity of salvation history. . . . The first part of this in time is meant to point to the second, the second to fulfil the first.'[28]

Peter Smulders puts it in this way: 'and in this man God's creative word is fully uttered and his plan of creation definitively accomplished by his saving act.'

To this point we have looked at God's 'making' in creation as one of creative and redemptive energy, interpreted through Christ as well as effected by him. To sum up: God's act of making is characterised by continuousness with immediacy, order with energy, the transcendent with the material, specific and local; the unchanging with the unforeseen. We have found it necessary to grope for phrases which suggest an inherent and particular quality of 'life' and of 'event'; and in order to meet the mystery of the Christ who is both agent of creation and himself incarnate, we have identified the power of his life or event in terms of that 'self-emptying' which is the only 'true creative act'.[29] We have noted, too, the paradox not in creation merely, but also in the Incarnation and the Crucifixion as being expressions of 'glory'.

The 'Word' as the agent of judgment.

To some extent these are all theological truisms, but it is necessary for our purpose to hold them in mind together, and they do not sit easily with each other:

'It is easy in one sense to see in the cosmic Christ of, say, the Colossian hymn, "the power in which the world intrinsically coheres" (Pannenberg); it is less easy to see that same power in the historical and resurrected Jesus. For it is in the *history* – resurrection – that the new thing God does, and the *discontinuity* between the old and new, are most easily seen; while it is in the "*metaphysics*", the theological truth of the creation and preservation and redemption of the world through Christ, that the *continuity* is most often observed.'[30]

This difficulty in holding together apparently discontinuous truths is eased, I think, when we look at the third aspect of God's activity in 'making'. God's making is creative; it is redemptive. Relating the one to the other is a third inherent quality, implied in the repeated phrase in Genesis 1, 'And God saw. . . . that it was good.'[31] This is the act of 'judging' which is part of the divine act of 'making'[32], and like the other elements in it, continuous and yet specific. Gustav Aulen reminds us that the acts by which God makes himself felt are classified in Christian language under three heads: creation, judgment and redemption. Just as the first and third have been completed and yet are continuous, so is the second. All three, that is, refer to the act of God in history and *also in the continuous present*:

'Behold, now is the acceptable time; behold, now is the day of salvation.'[33]

Aulen glosses this 'now is the day of creation, now is the day of judgment.' Christ the Word is, therefore, agent and interpretation of all three, including that of judgment, in their continuity and their immediacy. Aulen speaks of God's acts of creation, judgment and redemption as ever-continuing and of the relation of this his three-fold activity to the here and now.[34] The 'judgmental' aspect of Christ the Word in the activity of God's making, therefore, is crucial to our understanding. For it is this which lends urgency to the material and immediate aspect of creation:

'This is the power of the Word, and it is dangerous. Every word – even every idle word – will be accounted for at the day of judgment, *because the word itself has power to bring to judgment.* It is of the nature of the word to reveal itself and incarnate itself – to assume material form. Its judgment is, therefore, an intellectual but also a material judgment.'[35]

When we concentrate too exclusively on creation and redemption as the obverse and reverse of God's act of 'making', forgetting that 'judgment' relates to each, we lose that which gives them a special quality of coherence, and which by its paradox gives them particular human significance. Moreover, we do little service to the positive and essential aspects of God's judgmental activity in 'making', by too quickly subsuming that judgmental element in the redemptive. Judgment is an aspect of his making to be apprehended in its own power, and not as a movement existing only in order to create its own analgesic in salvation.

The creating of human creativity

Since this three-fold activity relates to the 'here and now', it follows that God's creative energy does not eliminate or pre-empt the creative activity of the creature: rather, it brings it about. Schoonenberg comments, 'God creates a world coming into being by bringing itself about'; and this is in line with the view of creation expressed by Jurgen Moltmann, who suggests that there is an 'open-ended' perfectible aspect to creation which allows it to choose to affirm that in which it mirrors its Creator.[36] Creation at its beginning establishes the possiblities of the ensuing history of salvation, and both creation and salvation history point towards the kingdom of glory.

The creative activity of the creature, therefore, can be expressed *artistically* as well as spiritually by the Augustinian doctrine of free will. The *posse non peccare* at the beginning of a creation becomes the *non posse peccare* of its proper completion; the *posse non mori* of that created is overcome by its *non posse mori*. In terms of the new creation which man the maker reflects, this means that the final consummation he describes in his art is one of 'eternal time', transience without tragedy, change without alteration, making without 'possessing'. It means we have Keat's *Ode to the Nightingale* without its tragic sense of waste. Melancholy's 'She dwells with Beauty, Beauty that must die' is here put into a new perspective and so transformed.

It was something of this which Walter de la Mare expressed in his vision of heaven's flowers which were shadowless; not shadowed, that is, by the passing hours of the sun:

'The loveliest thing earth hath, a shadow hath,
A dark and livelong hint of death,
Haunting it ever till its last faint breath.
Who then may tell
The beauty of heaven's shadowless asphodel?'[37]

The point of this is that the activity of man and his whole world (within that drama of choice, refusal and forgiveness which is the creaturely response to the 'making of God') is a creative one called forth as much by God's judgmental action as by his creative and redemptive one. Man's art expresses it as vitally as – though in terms different from – his morality. Schoonenberg sums it up by suggesting that God's 'making' involves 'not just this material creation but man as person and freedom, who realises himself and freely affirms, fetches in and perfects himself and his world around him. Man is created precisely in his free act.'

This kind of thinking, which sees man's creaturely activity as inherently creative, and as springing out of the kind of creation he is (which itself is determined by the kind of making which gave him being) chimes well with certain philosophical views of God the Maker recently put forward. O'-Donoghue, for instance, writes, 'if the creator is essentially creative then it is this creativity which constitutes the creature'.[38] And conversely,

'The creature can only participate in creation if there is a final ground of this activity: otherwise all agency, all creativity, falls away into nothingness. A true sharing in creation is possible only if this is first of all a true creation.'[39]

T. S. Eliot, who has perhaps best in this century expressed in poetry this relationship between the creativity of the Creator and the creativity of his created, put it this way:

'The Lord who created must wish us to create
And empty our creation again in his service
Which is already his service in creating.'[40]

O'Donoghue commented, 'if the being's essential nature is to give and share infinitely, this is what the act of "making" is.'

The act of making.

'. . . This is what the act of making is.' We are brought, finally, to look at the theology of human making, not as an act of self-aggrandisement, but in relation to the divine making which is its source. Moltmann has well reminded us of both an essential distinction (which the Hebrews perceived sharply and never ceased to insist on: that the Old Testament term for the creative activity of God, 'bara', is never used of the creative activity of man) and also of the points of similarity:

'It is used exclusively to describe the divine activity and is never used for the works of men. . . . The creative God plays with his own possibilities and creates out of nothing that which pleases him. Man can only play with something, which in turn is playing with him. He cannot play with nothing . . . . He can only play with love. Still, there are points of contact.'[41]

(Elsewhere Moltmann has pointed to the emphasis of the use of 'bara' in salvation acts in history, rather than in creation, though the term appears there also. Effectively, therefore, creation is a new act of salvation and salvation a new act of creation.)

This recognition of 'points of contact' between the human and the divine 'making' is, of course, that usually termed 'analogy', and allows man's creativity to be truly and and formally creation, as is God's, though with 'all due proportions guarded'.[42] One way in which 'the proportions are guarded' is to recognise that human creativity *cannot quite* initiate new being, since it is finite and relative. It has to have something on which to work. It is this which Karl Barth emphasises:

'The great unlikeness of the work of God in face of that of the creature consists in the fact that as the work of the Creator in the preservation and over-ruling of the creature the work of God takes the form of an absolute positing, a form which can never be proper to the work of the creature. But at the same time the divine work in relation to the creature also has the form of a conditioning, determining and altering of that which already exists. And inasmuch as the conditioning of another also belongs to the creaturely activity there is a certain similarity between the divine and the creaturely work. In view of this likeness and unlikeness, unlikeness and likeness, we can and should speak of a similarity, or comparableness, and therefore an analogy between the divine activity and the human. We have to speak of an *analogia operationis*.'[43]

. . . .'We can and should speak of a similarity.' How does this affect our view of the writer's task?

We have already seen that what distinguishes human 'making' from divine making is the need for material on which to work, and of this, more later. It follows that where it is analogous to divine making, where it 'conditions' or 'shapes' or 'alters', theologically it should at its highest answer to the same laws we have seen operating in God's 'making'. That is, it should bring to bear upon that material to which it responds, energies that are at once creative, judgmental and redemptive. In it there will be a sense of continuance, in which eternity intersects with time in the immediacy of the present artistic moment. There will be a sense of energy, vitality, contained within an overall orderliness which gives sense or coherence to the 'event' precipitated in the work of art itself. There will be a sense of the known and the forever familiar crossing with the unexpected and the unforeseen. There will, finally, be the effecting within the reader of a self-giving which enables him to enter into an understanding of self-emptying or self-forgetfulness as the ultimate creative act, in recognising the reality of something 'other'. All these will be welded together in an experience which is one of glory and joy.

The artist as benefactor.

It is when we begin to recognise these as the theological grounding of the human artist's making that we begin also to recover the Coleridgean idea of writer or artist as *'benefactor'*,[44] an emphasis not noticeably fashionable in the twentieth century. When he practises his art at its highest and humblest, in the context of these laws of making we have identified, that is what the artist's calling is. Barth found such a 'maker' in Mozart:

> 'I must again revert to Wolfgang Amadeus Mozart. Why is it that this man is so incomparable? Why is it that for the receptive, he has produced . . . music which for the true Christian is not mere entertainment, enjoyment or edification, but food and drink; music full of comfort and counsel for his needs. . . always "moving", free and liberating because wise, strong and sovereign? Why is it possible to hold that Mozart has a place in theology, especially in the doctrine of creation and also in eschatology. . . .? It is possible to give him this position because he knew something about creation in its total goodness – 1756–1791! This was the time when God was under attack for the Lisbon earthquake, and theologians. . . . were hard put to it to defend him. In face of the problem of theology, Mozart had the peace of God which far transcends all the critical or speculative reason that praises or reproves. . . .

He had heard, and causes those who have ears to hear. . . . the whole context of providence. As though in the light of this end, he heard the harmony of creation to which the shadow also belongs but on which the shadow is not darkness. . . . But the light shines all the more brightly because it breaks forth from the shadow. The sweetness is also bitter and cannot therefore cloy. Life does not fear death but knows it well. *Et lux perpetua lucet* (sic!) *eis* – even the dead of Lisbon. Mozart saw this light no more than we do, but he heard the whole world of creation enveloped by this light. Hence. . . . he heard the negative only in and with the positive. Yet in their inequality he heard them both together, as, for example, in the Symphony in G Minor of 1788. . . . Hearing creation unresentfully and impartially, he did not produce merely his own music but that of creation, its two-fold and yet harmonious praise of God. . . . He simply offered himself as the agent by which little bits of horn, metal and catgut could serve as the voices of creation, sometimes leading, sometimes accompanying, and sometimes in harmony. . . . He drew music from them all, expressing even human emotions in the service of this music, and not vice versa. He himself was only an ear for this music, and its mediator to other ears. . . . He died in misery like an "unknown soldier", and in company with Calvin, and Moses in the Bible, he has no known grave. But what does this matter? What does a grave matter when a life is permitted simply and unpretentiously, and therefore serenely, authentically and impressively, to express the good creation of God, which also includes the limitation and end of man?

. . . . In the music of Mozart. . . . we have clear and convincing proof that it is a slander on creation to charge it with a share in chaos because it includes a Yes and a No, as though orientated to God on the one side and nothingness on the other. Mozart causes us to hear, that even on the latter side, and therefore in its totality, creation praises its Master and is therefore perfect.'[45]

In such a view, man the maker properly produces works of art which both are *about* the work of judgment and salvation in creation, and also are themselves helping to effect it in the ongoing work of creation. The artist is seen, that is, as a mediator of that salvation which is God's: is seen as, through his work at its best, the mediator of that which God himself expresses in his creative activity: judgment and redemption.

There must be a source.

How may this be? There are one or two lines of thought in connection with it that I would like to sketch out (rather than develop). The first, which looks at the mode of the *activity* of the artist, has been well expressed by David Jones. He has suggested that all writings involve a 'remembering'[46], a re-presenting: what he calls an 'anamnesis':

'They show forth, re-call, discover and re-present those things that have belonged to men frbm the beginning.'[47]

'Re-present' is an interesting word, suggesting as it does at one and the same time an 'imitation' of that which is remembered and *a re-creation of its life, its experience*. It is no mere 'copy' of life Jones is adducing, but a re-vivifying of it so that it 'becomes here and now operative by its effects'. He argues also for the essential intersection in art of time with eternity:

'It is axiomatic that the function of the artist is to make through *sub specie aeternitatis*, but the works of man, unless they are of "now" and "of this place", can have no "for ever".'[48]

Such judgmental and saving powers as the writer uses, therefore, in his creative 'making', are grounded not finally in any self-induced creativity – vividly though that exists – as in that which gave it initial life. O'Donoghue put this very movingly:

'Creativity at whatever level is affirmation of the Other, a giving of being, a sharing. *Actio fit in passio*: the activity of the agent is *in* the other, *is* the other as brought into being. But the other is in turn a centre of action and creativity. The picture, the song, the poem has its own life and its own activity, and so with all the works of men.

The gift is the giving that is given. What is shared is itself a sharing. . . . Man the maker is a free flowing that goes on and on, to infinity.

But there is a source. There must be a source. For if all agency is the giving of agency, so, conversely, all agency is the receiving of agency. For the source must also be the ground here and now. The creator is present here and now in all creative agency.'[49]

(We may compare David Jones: 'All art is a sign of the form-making activities predicated of the Logos. It is then the form-making that causes man's art to be bound to God'[50]: and S. T. Coleridge: 'The primary imagination I hold to be the living power and prime agent of all human perception, and as a repetition in the finite mind of the eternal act of creation in the infinite I AM'.[51]).

Not only is God the Maker the source of that giving, that 'free flowing' which is man's 'making' in art and literature: the *material* which man must have in order to create is that very creative activity of God we have described earlier. For we have seen that man's creaturely creative response is to God's creative, judging and redeeming 'making'. *And this means, quite simply, that the material of man's creative acts is God's creation, God's judgment and God's salvation.* It is these to which man responds, and from which his art flows. It is, after all, the only material available to him.

We should, I think, take very seriously the freedom inherent in this. Art arises from the involvement of man in the divine drama of 'choice, refusal and salvation' as we saw earlier. Hence, literature which seriously responds to the judgment of God by *rejecting* its apparent injustice: or which reflects the fury and distress of the creature finding itself in a universe whose spiritual laws seem distorted: or which grieves over the dereliction of man in the wilderness: all these, as the Book of Job showed us, can be the source of valid and responsible artistic 'makings' by men, in response to the material with which they find themselves. That is why books like *Waiting for Godot* or *King Lear* have such compelling artistic power. They are a literature of refusal.

Delight.

But the Book of Job reminds us of one thing more, which perhaps colours all the rest. That is, the 'glory', the joy, the 'felicity' of creation, touched on earlier, and perhaps the final truth about all artistic 'making'. The Old Testament reiterates constantly the beauty and joy of creation. God's work in it is seen as ultimately for delight: 'and behold, it was very good.'[52] And it is the peculiar nature of this joy inherent in man's making with which I want to conclude this chapter, for its implication both for the role of the writer and our critical assessments of his work is immense. Helen Oppenheimer has pointed out that 'felicity', 'happiness', itself an essential ingredient in any creation-eschatology, is of extraordinary aesthetic power. 'Beauty penetrating into song' gives a form of disclosure which flat statement or narration cannot.[53] She cites as an example the extra narrative element at the conclusion of the Book of Job (the 'happy ending') which, even if 'tacked-on' as some have argued, is self-authenticated in its disclosure of glory, of 'blessing which goes with the grain of the universe'. It is the same disclosure of which Jeremiah speaks:

'Thy words were found, and I ate them, and thy words became to me a joy and the delight of my heart. . . .'[54]

One aspect of this joy, delight, in 'making' is its ordering, making coherent, of that which initially has no extension: 'What was *inanis et vacua* became radiant with form.'[55] But another and profounder element in it is that such 'making' has no end beyond itself, creating for delight: 'The wisdom of God is saying, "I was daily his delight, rejoicing (playing) before him always." ' The Knox translation of this runs, 'I made play in this world of dust, with the sons of Adam for my playing fellows.'[56] 'Play' is the activity of man living creatively for pure delight: such an existence is itself a 'making' and informs the highest art of which man is capable: one in which he shares his play with God. For in it participation in the divine making is as full, as creative, as judging and as redemptive as human 'making' can ever be. Moltmann comments:

> 'Man is to give glory to the true God and rejoice in God's and his own existence, for this by itself is meaning enough. . . . Anyone who lays hold of the joy which embraces the Creator and his own existence also gets rid of the dreadful question of existence: for what?'[57]

As T. S. Eliot wrote, 'The essential advantage for a poet is not to have a beautiful world with which to deal: it is to be able to see beneath both beauty and ugliness; to see the boredom, and the honour, and the glory.'[58]

I have said that such human 'making' participates as fully as is possible for finite beings in the nature of divine making, and that this involves the judging and redemptive activities also. For, of course, it is here that the supremely creative act is found to be one of self-abnegation. Helen Oppenheimer insists that the joy expressed through aesthetic arises from affirming life, even within the experience of dereliction: the dereliction is redeemable because it is grounded within God, not within oneself. A suffering *God*, that is, is essnetial to the concept of joy inherent in 'making'. For, as we saw earlier, that which the Giver *is* the power to give, since it is of his own being that he gives. It is a giving of giving, a sharing of sharing. If the being's essential nature is to give and share infinitely, that is what the act of 'making' is. Human making differs in that its capacity is not infinite in the one sense of giving or sharing *ex nihilo*. It has to receive in order to give or share.[59] When the human 'maker' abandons the little idea of memorialising himself, and even perhaps the idea, slightly more generous, of memorialising some other, at the heart of his 'making' he finds the need to 'die' through his art[60]: to empty himself in order to make glory. As T. S. Eliot has argued (see Giles Gunn's discussion of this):

'In order for the poem – or any work of literature – to achieve its true character as an autonomous, objective entity. . . . the poet must sacrifice his personal desires and intentions to the formal requirements of his art. . . . the very gesture of poetic utterance thus becoming the representative religious act.'[61]

In emptying himself to make glory, the artist not only witnesses to the glory of God's 'making', but co-operates with it and is himself, in judgment and healing, a mediator of it:

'Follow, poet, follow right
To the bottom of the night,
With your unconstraining voice
Still persuade us to rejoice:

With the forming of a verse
Make a vineyard of the curse,
Sing of a human unsuccess
In a rapture of distress;

In the deserts of the heart
Let the healing fountain start,
In the prison of his days
Teach the free man how to praise.'[62]

CHAPTER FOUR

The critical context: a use and abuse of Christian criticism

So far we have been looking primarily at theological aspects of the critical exercise. I suggested early in this study that there were strong reasons for the necessity of this. Amongst the most important of these are certain characteristics of the practice of criticism itself, and it is these we must next examine. What is the proper study of a critic? To whom does he address himself, on what subject and with what intention? Only when one has looked at these questions it is then possible to examine whether there can properly be the exercise of such a function within a framework that is Christian: a 'Christian criticism' in the sense that a Christian world view is its matrix.

It is arguable, of course, and with some justification, that all this is much ado about nothing, that critics have always examined and always will, the subject of their appraisal for their own personal baseline. Hence the considerable divergence between critics, not to say acrimony (see below, *passim*) about both their task and the criteria to be brought to bear within it. True. But as I suggested earlier, bitter war is currently joined (and looks like continuing) over the whole nature of the critical activity in particular relation to its social, political, philosophical and moral referrents. At such a moment it would seem irresponsible for a Christian critic to duck the issue and not to examine where he stands vis-a-vis such questions, and why. And until he has located what is definable about his own activity as a critic he will be in poor case to take part in the debate at all.

Critical concerns.

What, then, does a critic study and for what purpose? I quoted earlier[1] M. V. Abrams's classic exposition of the four heads of critical concern as exemplified in the developing history of criticism: the subject (the 'universe'), the audience, the artist, and the work. Professor Abrams identified the shifting of emphasis from one to the other of these concerns as helping to determine the developments in critical practice. While in every period attention is paid to all four, there is almost always recognisably a dominance of one element over the other three. The dominating element tends to suggest what is the critic's current understanding of the nature and purpose of literature itself.

Mimesis, content-orientated criticism, and 'truth'.

Where, for instance, it is the subject matter which is of primary concern to the critical reader we have a view of literature that is Aristotelian and 'mimetic', or 'representational'. The task of the creative writer is seen as that of recording faithfully and accurately both the external universe and (later in history) the inner world of man. His fidelity in this is the basic measure of his art. Catherine Belsey has pointed out how strongly this view of the function of literature has persisted, from Aristotle to our own day: and quotes Ruskin, for instance, as very clearly defining, within the modern period, how the 'world of thought' is an aspect of mimesis even as is the natural world. 'Truth to nature' is the first and highest essential and mimetic accuracy is the foundation of all art:

'Although it is possible to reach what I have stated to be the first end of art, the representation of facts, without reaching the second, the representation of thoughts, yet it is altogether

impossible to reach the second without having previously
reached the first. . . .

. . . .Nothing can atone for want of truth. . . . (and therefore) I
shall look only for truth; bare, clear, downright statement of
facts; showing in each particular, as far as I am able, what the
truth of nature is, and then seeking for the plain expression of
it.'[2]

By the time Ruskin affirmed this strong view of mimesis as
the controlling element in assessing literature, critical practice
in England had already shifted twice in its emphases, and I
refer to his comments primarily to show the continuing
strength of the mimetic – or as some would call it, the 'realistic' – view of literature. In our own late twentieth century,
as David Lodge has pointed out, the same view holds its
ground. He quotes John Bayley, writing in 1968, on the
'realistic' novel:

'It is the *point* about the novel. . . . that it is social intercourse
by other means. Its unprecedented flux of words is concerned –
as Tolstoy said – with questions of how men live and should
live. . . . *It is a sharing of the commonplace* through the medium
of the exceptional man, the medium of the artist-novelist.'[3]

Ruskin's 'facts' and 'truth of nature' are here primarily social,
the 'commonplaces' of reality, but the thrust is the same.

Yet this mimetic view is under intense and increasing pressure, and that quite apart from the shifts to dominance of the
'audience' and the 'artist' in critical thinking. Perhaps the
clearest indication of the difficulty is in the necessary assertion
of a relationship with 'truth' that the mimetic theory involves.
For how if there be no such thing as 'truth'?

'If there is no single Truth about the world for the writer to
identify and transcribe, then neither is there a single Truth
about a text for the critic to identify and transcribe.'[4]

It will at once be obvious from this that questions about

whether a work of art is 'true' to the world it 'reflects' or 'creates' raise further questions about whether that 'world' does indeed have any 'truth' and even if it has, whether that truth can be known. And such questions inevitably put at risk any notion of critical practice as *itself* asserting a relationship with truth and thereby establishing an authoritative stance:

> 'The critic experiences before the book the same linguistic conditions as does the writer before the world. . . .; (his task) is not to discover forms of truth, but forms of "validity".'[5]

This last comment, by Roland Barthes, is a very characteristic utterance from the 'new formalist' school of 'structuralist' critics of whom I shall be saying more later. Sufficient here to note that the focus of the criticism has here become the *work itself*: to this we shall move in due course.

Pragmatic, audience-orientated criticism: instruction and delight.
John Bayley, in his attack on the 'new formalists' from which I quoted above, referred to his reading of a novel as 'social intercourse by other means'. In so doing he was fusing two critical emphases: that of mimesis or representation of the known social world, and that of delighting, instructing, educating or improving the audience of readers.

This shift of thinking about literature, which sees it as primarily purposive rather than primarily imitative, is clearly discernible in Sir Philip Sidney's *The Apologie for Poetry*, the first classic of English criticism[6] written some time in the early 1580's:

> 'Poesy therefore. . . . is an arte of imitation. . . . figuring foorth. . . with this end, to teach and delight.'[7]

It is readily apparent that for Sidney the imitation is *in order* to delight, and the delight is *in order* to instruct, for 'right poets' are those who 'delight to move men to take that goodness in hande, which without delight they would flye as from a stranger.'[8] The critical emphasis, that is, falls upon what is happening to the audience as a result of the work under survey, rather than what is the integral value of the work within its own artistic terms. Writing is not an end in itself, but a social or moral function.

This emphasis in critical thinking is again discernible in strength through to our own day, though its formulations are extraordinarily diverse. At the beginning of the modern period Matthew Arnold is perhaps the most characteristic critic in this perspective, arguing for a high view of literature because it is surrogate for the now discredited religious faith of the West. More recently Marxist critics would argue that literature is the potential pattern for the class struggle[9], both in its dialectic structure and in its potentially revolutionary iconoclastic power. Less narrowly, the 'socialising' function of literature is urged by writers as diverse as Doris Lessing and Arnold Wesker, whose comments we noted in chapter two; and, for instance, by Northrop Frye, after the 'New Critics' had rejected 'realism' (amongst other things) in the 1950's. The conflicts which fragment our society, Frye argues, most of them primarily class conflicts, can be subjected to the harmonising power of literature, since 'literary criticism, as part of a liberal education, can make it possible to conceive of a free and classless society, transcending the world we know, clear of the bondage of history':

'This criticism, autonomous and isolated, acts as a solvent for the class struggle, not in the world but in the imagination.'[10]

Among some recent developments in criticism, including that of structuralism, there is, at least implicitly, a rejection of 'social engineering' or moral education through literature. At one point, however, the focus upon the audience/readership element of critical discussion which lies behind the instructive or hedonistic theories of literature is extremely relevant to structuralist thought. This is in the recognition that the 'text' is inevitably open to some plurality of readings as long as the language in which it is created is the common property of both author and reader. I shall look further at this concept of 'reader-power' when we are discussing the kind of criticism which places the 'artist' at the centre of critical discussion. Sufficient here to draw attention to two important and relevant insights recent criticism has pressed upon us. First, that of Wimsatt, who (with M. G. Beardsley) in 1946 attacked 'the intentionalist fallacy of certain kinds of expressive criticism' and in so doing drew attention to the 'public' nature of language. Because the language was public the piece of writing or 'text' *belonged to the reading public*:

> 'The poem is not the critic's own and not the author's. . . . The poem belongs to the public. It is embodied in language, the peculiar possession of the public, and it is about the human being, an object of public knowledge.'[11]

We might note how this concept of language as 'public' is a fairly blunt instrument; we have already seen (in chapter two) that 'public' and 'private' use of language in literature intertwine, and we shall look at this when discussing authorial authority. But the emphasis on language as 'public' opens the way to 'reader-theory' – potentially valid plurality of reading based on the common possession of language by the writer and his readers.

It is, however, the 'structuralist' Stanley Fish who most powerfully puts the emphasis on the reader/audience. Catherine Belsey points out that for Fish the emphasis on the reading *experience* is fundamental. Reading is an activity, a process; meanings are 'events' in the reader's consciousness; the important question to ask of a text is what it *does*; and the proper procedure of the critic is

> 'an analysis of the developing responses of the reader in relation to the words as they succeed one another in time.'[12]

I have put some stress on this because, although generally this critical style has a sharply different background from the 'instructiveness' of Sidney's approach, yet in making the centre of critical consciousness whatever is happening to the readers he is following logically upon the instructive view; it is the ideological context which is different. And at the same time it is worth noting that this view of literature also recognises 'word as event', in a sense analogical to that we observed earlier in this study.[13]

Expressive, artist-centred criticism: the orbit of genius.

A difficulty attendant both in 'mimetic' centred criticism and that which focusses primarily on the effect of literature upon the audience/readership is that neither fully allows for the observably peculiar quality of the artist himself. His 'genius' or individual creative imagination is wholly answerable neither to an 'objective' natural and imitable reality observable by all and therefore inarguable, nor to the (supposedly more limited) vision of his readers. So we reach the critical perspective which attempts to correct this. In this view poetry is the 'spontaneous overflow of powerful feelings' of the gifted individual, or way of thinking 'in which the artist himself becomes the major element generating both the artistic product and the criteria by which it is to be judged.'[4] In such a view the writer is creating literature about *himself*, about his own mind and spirit, about his own responses to the external world rather than its universally observable qualities.

The effect of artist-centredness in critical thinking is, as John Stuart Mill observed, radical in a number of directions. 'Spontaneity' is of higher virtue than technical expertise; the external world is chiefly of virtue as the 'occasion for the generation of poetry'. Perhaps most important for all for us at this stage of our inquiry, the audience, far from being the centre of the critical debate, ceases to be of any importance at all.

'Poetry is feeling, confessing itself to itself in moments of solitude. . . . All poetry is of the nature of soliloquy.'[15]

75

The poet's audience, as Abrams points out, is reduced to a single member, consisting of the poet himself.

Further; not only is the audience's response unimportant, but the way that audience is *affected* is also of no concern. Indeed, Mill puts it more strongly still, suggesting that literature with an instructive or social end in view by that very condition ceases to be literature. When the writer's

> 'act of utterance is not itself the end, but the means to an end. . . . – to work upon the feelings or upon the belief, or the will, of another – when the expression of his emotions is tinged also by that purpose. . . . then it ceases to be poetry and becomes eloquence.'[16]

This is an unashamedly elitist view of literature. Its virtue is that it gives full freedom to that which is particular and idiosyncratic – the 'uniqueness' – of any work of art. In doing so it allows full play to that dynamic which Coleridge called the 'Imagination', without attempting to rationalise it in cultural or social terms. But it places the reader (insofar as he exists at all) entirely under the author's authority. We may notice the ambivalence of attitude here: John Keats, for instance, insisted that he 'never wrote one single line of Poetry with the least shadow of public thought'[17], but yet the unsympathetic and imperceptive reactions of the critical journals wounded and angered him deeply. What is required of the reader is a 'wonder' such as that adumbrated by Carlyle:

> 'Genuis has privileges of its own; it selects an orbit for itself; and be this never so eccentric, if it is indeed a celestial orbit, we mwere stargazers must at last compose ourselves; must cease to cavail at it, and begin to observe it, and calculate its laws.'[18]

Reader-theory criticism

What we have already seen of recent criticism seems sharply opposed to such a view. If language is a public possession, the reading an 'event' in the reader's mind, it follows that reader-theory criticism, or 'reader-power' (to quote a popular term for it) as an element in the critical enterprise, has some validity. In such a view the reader is as creatively engaged as the writer in the literary operation. Indeed, the debate has recently centred upon how far the author can be said to have *any* critical authority over the text. The mimetic or 'realistic' critical emphasis, the instructive or social emphasis, the subjective or idiosyncratic emphasis – all these had offered the text 'a single, determinate meaning, however, complex, and the authority for this meaning was the author.'[19] The 'New Critics', by contrast, such as Wimsatt and Cleanth Brooks, instituted the 'text itself' as the authority. But Northop Frye goes further, rejecting any quest even for an implicit intention on the part of the author in his work. The effect of this Catherine Belsey sees as 'liberating':

> 'Freed in this way from the tyranny of the author, and available for interpretation by a self-conscious and systematic criticism *which is independent of literature*, the text is inevitably plural, open to a number of readings.'[20]

This 'plurality of readings' could correspond to the plurality of readers: though Ms. Belsey recognises that there is a spectrum of critical ideas here, with at one extreme 'a new authority figure as guarantor of a single meaning, a timeless, transcendent, highly trained model reader who cannot be wrong', and at the other a 'general participation in the production of a plurality of meanings.'[21] Moreoever, implicit in those words I have placed in italics is a question about the relevance of the text as *literature* to the reader's view of it.

The problem lies in how far there is a 'meaning' safeguarded by the formal properties of the work, and inherent in the 'creative event' as the author experienced it; and whether the reader's 'event' in the reading activity complements this, or over-rules it. Further: who is the reader? A theoretical 'perfect' reader, fully informed on all relevant data? Or a multiplicity of readers? Is there such a person as a 'good reader'?

W. J. Slatoff inserts that there is, and that 'good readers and critics' are those who learn to 'submit' to the work and let their responses be 'directed and limited by it'.[22]

Stanley Fish, whose emphasis on the reading experience we looked at earlier, sees readers as 'participants in the construction of meaning'[23], but, as Catherine Belsey points out, fails to recognise the probability that a plurality of readers must necessarily produce a plurality of readings. Again his reader is a single, real reader 'who does everything he can to keep himself informed'.

On the importance of teaching reading.

There is a way through the apparent collision of views here, one that has important implications for us in this study. Underlying the whole debate is the question of authority, not only 'whose', but 'whether' – whether, that is, authority is available in the critical enterprise. Social and political ideologies sharpen the problem. George Steiner has perhaps put it best[24]:

'Even to face the issue of correlations between genuine literacy and an authoritarian value-structure, is to repudiate out of hand the. . . . cheery vulgarity of populist accent which characterises the current climate of cultural-educational argument in the West.'

Creative literacy, he argues, 'was always the disciplined, authoritatively transmitted possession of the few'; for,

' "Texts" are indeed inexhaustible to our needs, to that constant questioning and disinterested "irresponsibility" of fundamental provocation which engenders original thought. But "texts" are also initially and, sometimes, over a long period "closed".'

Reader-power, that is, to be valid, needs a basis of discipline, training and information: Steiner's 'reader' is a carefully selected and highly trained disciple, submissive to the text *and all that has gone to create it*:

'If we are serious about our business, *we shall have to teach reading*. We shall have to teach it from the humblest level of rectitude, the parsing of a sentence. . . all the way to that ideal of complete collaboration between writer and reader as set out by Peguy. We shall have to learn to proceed, step by step, frmm the near-dyslexia of current student reading-habits to that enigmatic act of penetrative elucidation, the sense of the passage being perceived and in fact "realised between the lines".'

This is not at all a rejection of reader-power. It is a demand that critical emphasis on reader rather than artist be taken so seriously that proper training prepares the reader-creator-critic for his task. For what is being 'authoritatively' handed down is 'the transmission of tensed delight before the word'. It is a felicity which artist and reader create together: the nature of the preparation for it, therefore, is of the most serious importance.

Objective, text orientated criticism; structure and technique.
Such a view of the 'mystery' of reading leads us to the fourth category of critical emphasis, that in which the 'work or the 'text' is at the centre. In brief, this emphasis leads us to a view of literature as existing for its own sake, freed of responsibility to audience, of representational accuracy, of elucidation through the sensibility of the artist. It is directly opposed to the classic concept that 'art imitates life and is therefore in the last analysis answerable to it. . . . making it better or at the least more bearable'.[25] The 'expressive' view of literature we have just noted, primarily associated with the Romantic movement, led almost inevitably to an overturning of the classic view, by suggesting that 'life imitates art'. That is, our perception of life, the ways we look at it, are shaped by our culture, the way artists and writers have made us 'see'. But in that case, what is art and literature *itself* about? What does it 'imitate', if not 'life'? The answer would be that all art is about art, all literature is about other literature:

'Poems are not made out of experience, they are made out of
poetry – that is, the tradition of disposing the possiblities of
language to poetic ends.'[26]

In such a critical perspective Milton could (to push this to the
absurd) be seen as 'passionately sincere' in his poem *Lycidas*
because he was 'deeply interested in the structure and symbolism of funeral elegies and had been practising since ado-
lescence on every fresh corpse in sight, from the university
beadle to the fair infant dying of a cough'.[27] It is the technical
structure of the writing which makes its 'art': not its accuracy
of observation, loftiness of vision, or effect for good on its
readership:

'Modern criticism has shown us that to speak of content as such
is not to speak of art at all, but of experience; and that it is
only when we speak of the *achieved* content, the form, that we
speak as critics. The difference between content, or experience,
and achieved content, or art, is technique.'[28]

*The 'new formalism' of the structuralists: the autonomy of
literature.*

This 'form' based criticism leads us directly to the work of
the structuralist critics, whose 'new formalism' or 'nouvelle
critique' begins from a view of literature as definable entirely
in terms of (primarily linguistic) structures. Its origins are
traceable in the interaction of Futurist poetry and Formalist
poetics in Russia immediately before and after the Revolution,
and it develops out of the semiotics (science of signs) of
Saussure and Jakobson.

The critic Roland Barthe's work is a helpful example of the
development of structuralist thought. Writing in 1953, he
suggested that a crisis of language (which had political origins)
was true for all literature, and that the activity of writing
could now no longer be seen as 'the process by which life was
turned into literature'; rather literature was recognisable and
to be valued for its complexity and difficulty: 'writing is now

to be saved not by virtue of what it exists for, but thanks to the work it has cost.'[29] By 1966 Barthes has developed this view radically. Language is not used by man to 'express' himself, but is itself, *in its use*, the defining activity of man. Thus,

> 'the field of the writer is nothing but writing itself, not as the pure "form" conceived by an aesthetic of art for art's sake, but much more radically, as the only area (espace) for the one who writes.'[30]

Hence the meaning of the writing activity is to substitute for the 'instance of reality' the instance of 'discourse', 'the writer being no longer one who writes *something*, but one who writes, absolutely'.[31]

Writing is thus an autonomous activity relating to nothing beyond itself. Behind this view lies Saussure's study of semiotics, with its emphasis on the arbitrariness of the relationship between the 'acoustic image' and that which it signifies. A verbal sign or word is the union of this 'signifier' and the 'signified': and if their relationship is arbitrary, then so is the 'word' which by cultural agreement embodies that relationship. There is, therefore, what David Lodge calls a 'nucleus of arbitrariness at the heart of language'.[32] This is obviously of the greatest importance; it follows that it is the relationship (i.e. the differences) *between words* which makes for communication, rather than their reference to objects or the concepts the words denote. Hence the important aspect for the critic of the act of writing is not the accuracy of the words in representing, acting as signs for, something else: but rather in the complex relationship of the words *to each other*. The linguistic patterning is significant in itself, with no reference beyond itself. Thus it is that for structuralists:

> 'The linguistic reference of words is words. . . . texts refer to nothing but other texts.'[33]

From this it follows that there is no such thing as the 'subject' of a piece of writing: it has dissolved, disappeared, proved to be only 'one level' of the activity of interpretation. The 'structure' of the discourse is all.

As David Lodge has pointed out, we stand here at the point of apparent collison between quite different philosophical traditions, and the debate cannot well proceed 'without moving from the area of literature and criticism to that of philosophy'.[34] For the outline of critical views I have sketched above suggests that critical perspectives like the 'mimetic' or the 'instructive' are based on a perception of reality as fundamentally coherent and orderly, i.e. as having a 'truth'; whereas the critical perspective of structuralism claims no relationship with any such 'reality' but is self-defining, and is adjusted to a view of life as fundamentally random and arbitrary.

It is in this context that I would turn our thinking again to the theological discussion of the earlier part of this study. I want to suggest that in this theology we might find not only the model of creative activity which is the artist's making' we looked at earlier: but also a solvent for our current critical dilemmas and confrontations.

The critical resolution.

It is T. S. Eliot, again, who gives us a lead here, and I am indebted to Denis Donoghue's penetrating essay on his work in identifying certain key concepts. Donoghue reminds us of a contrast in the use of words which relates strongly to the critical dissensions we have just examined. The first use of words, which he calls 'classical', emphasises that seamless web of relations in which both language and that Nature it enacts are seen as coherent and connected. The second use, which he labels 'modern', calls into question any connectedness inherent in either Nature or the words we use, insisting that 'every relation must be invented as though the word has just begun. . . In modern poems the words are independent and therefore lonely.'[35]

This modern consciousness, one of fragmentation and 'absence in reality', seems to me to be the 'creative' obverse of the structuralists' critical reverse. For both, word-use is arbitrary and must be self-proving. There is no anterior coherence to provide generic relationship.

But T. S. Eliot goes beyond both the serene connectedness of the 'classical' mode and the isolation and arbitrariness of the modern, to find in language itself power and aura, *though it be of words existing in a void*; it is a critique whose theology is that of the Word:

> 'The life of a soul does not consist in the contemplation of one consistent world but in the painful task of unifying. . . joining incompatible ones, and passing, when possible, from two or more discordant viewpoints to a higher which shall somehow include and transmute them.'[36]

The means which Eliot adopts to achieve this inclusive and transmuting view is, to quote Donoghue, 'language itself, issuing from a perspective grander even than Tiresias: language itself, increasingly in Eliot identified with the Word of God.'

It is because Eliot has identified this theological concept of language as a basis for criticism that he can contain the final oppositions of, for instance, the sense of the arbitrariness of reality and the affirmation of its coherence and ultimacy; or the abyss of timelessness and the common and burdening sense of time. In Donoghue's summary of this he takes us to the very heart of a view of language that is theological:

> 'Nearly everything in Eliot's language can be explained by his feeling that the truth of things resides in an indeterminate area: neither subject nor object, but a state compounded of both; neither time nor eternity, but a state in which the double obligation is registered; neither men nor God, but a being, conceivable in words but not in fact, who is vouched for not in identifiable speech but in language itself, eventually to be invoked as Logos.'[37]

What is in view here is a vision which, far from *denying* the arbitrariness perceived by the structuralists, accommodates it but subsumes it within a profounder understanding which perceives an 'ultimate Reality', a God, even within the void itself. It is, of course, a reiterated vision within the Bible, from Genesis to Job to the Gospel accounts of the Crucifixion. In the final chapter of this study we shall examine this more fully.

Further: if for a critic the 'truth of things thus resides' in 'neither men nor God, but a being. . . . vouched for in language itself, eventually to be invoked as Logos', then the critic's task and the creator's are seen to be the obverse and reverse of the same activity, answering to the same final laws and moved by the same dynamism.

Abuses of a Christian criticism.

It remains to identify what might be the qualities of a criticism rooted in such a Christian theology. What will be its inherent and observable patterns? It may perhaps be a useful exercise to begin by clearing away certain widely held false assumptions, by identifying what such a Christian criticism is not. It is, first, essential to recognise that a criticism with so high a view of language as that touched on above will never 'violate proper method by a prior dogmatic'.[38] To do so would be to force upon the language structure before one a false coherence, not allowing the vitality of its own 'relatedness' to be discovered. Giles Gunn has commented that the value of a criticism rooted in Christian theology is in no way:

> 'to subsume literature under some doctrinal umbrella. . .
> (turning) literature to some ideological or apologetic use which
> is rarely if even appropriate to it.'[39]

To force upon a text such a reading would be to respect neither its representational truth nor its instructive or hedonistic purpose nor its authorial authority nor its textual integrity: it would be, rather, a tyranny of readership. There is a

splendid *reductio ad absurdum*, by Robert Conquest, of this
supposed Christian critical method, in a 1963 issue of *The
Critical Quarterly*, in which he presents satirically an apparently seriously intended critical analysis of Kingsley Amis's
Lucky Jim. Space forbids the quotation of more than a short
extract here, but the whole is well worth reading:

> 'Dixon, the hero, is of course Everyman. In this capacity he is
> able (or required) to represent the whole human race (from
> Eskimo, page 97, to Roman, page 255) – and even to indicate
> the transcendental and universal scope of the Godhead by
> becoming briefly a Martian (page 92). (This reminds us
> ineluctably – and, as we shall see, importantly – of C. S.
> Lewis's religious fiction.)

> But, and far more to our purpose, Dixon is also the Son of
> Man. The surname, with the Cross at its centre for him to *Di(e)
> on*, is among the more overt and conscious of the many signs
> the author has scattered. The name Jim instantly brings to
> mind the words of the Epistle of St. James. . . .

> In a general way, the conflict between the powers of darkness
> and of light is the "plot" of the novel. It is not here my
> purpose to examine its scriptural ramifications. It is sufficient to
> note such cruxes as the strikingly obvious beginning of chapter
> 6, so extraordinary and exaggerated in the *apparent* context of a
> mere awakening, but so essential in the basic religious context –
> DIXON WAS ALIVE AGAIN – and so on, throughout. For
> example, in Dixon's "lecture" we naturally find the Sermon on
> the Mount, though there are other elements such as St. Paul's
> "speaking with tongues". (It may also be significant that in the
> film version, Dixon gets his finger caught in the lectern: that is,
> finds himself in effect bound to the wooden upright with a
> crosspiece – an obvious enough crucifixion symbol.)

> Again, it is in accord with tradition that mortals in a state of
> extreme sin are unable to pronounce the holy name. We find
> that the porter (page 92) – described flatly as "a very bad man"
> – is unable to use Dixon's correct name, and he substitutes
> "Jackson" on the analogy of the various "odds" and "bobs"
> used in old expletives instead of God. (The first syllable may

represent some faint memory of the Jewish Jehovah-Yahweh substitution.)

We also cannot fail to note the pervasive echoes or representations of the archangels. The friendly Michie is an obvious Michael. But who can Bertrand be? The name means "bright raven" (*Origins of British Chrisitan Names* by J. P. Ogilvie, London, 1928, page 13), and we at once recall the black-winged being, formerly a representation of all light and still bearing the name Lucifer, but now an evil spirit par-excellence. . . .'[40]

What is particularly joyous in this satire is its linking together of two related critical faults: on the one hand the wresting of the text under scrutiny to the pre-disposition of the critic's own view *regardless* of the tone, nature, idiom and quality of Amis's book: and on the other hand the display of pointless pedantry, of learned references totted up for the edification of the reader, with no real relevance to the work in hand. In both cases Robert Conquest is pillorying the critic who remakes the novel or play or poem in his own image, without humility before the writing as a work of imagination, with its own unique organisation which can only be illuminated by an attention to what it totally expresses. This is 'reader-power' indeed, an excellent example of its absurdity when the *reader* is autonomous.

The abuse inherent in such an approach arises primarily from the grounding of the text under discussion in an imposed theology, instead of such a theology determining for the critic his understanding of language potential. It is on the whole not the task of a criticism rooted in Christian theology to concern itself only or even primarily with 'religious' elements in literature; only, or even primarily, with 'content'. Rather, its task is to bring to the critical enterprise a characteristic and challenging vision of what the nature and dimensions of that critical enterprise can be.

Characteristics of a Christian criticism.

If the theology of the Logos as a ground for criticism can be presented as an adequate solvent for many of the critical disputes noted above, then it ought to be possible to identify the characteristics of such a 'Christian criticism' which help validate this claim. We have already observed Eliot's perception of the arbitrariness of language contained within the dynamic stability of Logos. This is paradox: and it is perhaps the capacity for paradox in theologically grounded criticism which is its most characteristic and valuable quality. Walter Stein summed this up in his description of an (idealised) Christian critic:

> 'Because of his doctrinal commitment his vision will always be
> framed with orthodoxy, but because this orthodoxy centres
> upon the doctrine of the incarnation, *the reality of both spirit and
> flesh*, their opposition and their oneness, their degradation and
> divine renewal; because it is both personalist and societal and
> because in proportion to the authenticity of its faith it is itself
> intimately exposed to the pressures of unbelief, this framework
> is forever open to fresh disclosures of experience; at once
> traditionalist and revolutionary, permanently engaged on
> assimilating the shocks and pressures and the exaltations of the
> unceasing flux of change.'[41]

That is, there is an accommodation of opposition, an inherent dialectic in the very nature of the theology which provides the grounding. It is *both* stable *and* open to fresh disclosures: both conserving and subversive.

And this becomes the more important when we recognise that many of the critical controversies which have engaged us in these pages relate not only to opposed world views but to the dialectical nature of art itself. For every work of art resists final explication: it is always beyond rationalisation. There is in its very identity that which makes it possible for critics to read it, validly, in totally different ways, and to express quite differently, not the work of art itself, but what is visible *in* that work of art.

Dame Helen Gardner has expressed this most helpfully in her book *Religion and Literature*, when she borrows from Professor Gombuch's book, *Art and Illusion*, his account of the different ways we can read a visual image. She used the diagram of a folded sheet of paper. When we first glimpse it, some of us will see the AA folds projecting nearest us; others will see the BB lines in that way:

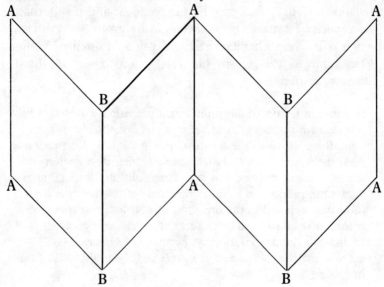

But, as Dame Helen points out:

> 'Whichever way we read it at first sight, with a little effort and some practice we can switch from one reading to the other; *but we can never see both interpretations at once*, nor can we even see any intermediate possibilities. . . This little problem where there is no "right way" to read the image can provide an analogy with the literary critical situation.'[42]

This account of a *visual* image helps us to seize on the apparently mutually incompatible truths of literature and the criticism that attends it. Such a richness of 'image' is available both in the nature of the literary art and in the kind of theology we have been looking at. There is, in the paradoxical nature of Christian theology an adequate referent for the ambiguity of much literature, where the very nature of its characteristic structures is not only being given scope, but is analogically inherent in Christian understanding.

There is one other characteristic of that criticism which roots itself in theology to which we ought to pay special attention, and that is its quality of 'judgment'. Popularly speaking, this characteristic is often thought of as the defining *function* of a Christian criticism, which is too often made synonymous with censorship. I want to say much more in the concluding chapter about the theology of judgment which helps shape the judgmental function of the critic; but at this point it would be more helpful to look at the issue in terms of the critical task.

'Judgment' as a critical activity.

We might begin by noting that when writers and critics seem to be at odds with each other it is often because either the criticism has been divorced from literature and understood to be a separate enterprise: or, more frequently, because the critic is felt to be conducting his task in so pejoratively 'judgmental' a way that the artist feels himself professionally maltreated and humiliated and his work accordingly diminished. That same John Osborne, whose sallies illuminated some of our earlier thinking in this study, put it like this:

'MRS. JAMES:
(INTERVIEWER)   What would you say was the function of critics, if any?

WYATT:
(WRITER)   Critics are sacrosanct. You must make it clear to your readers that they are simply and obviously more important than poets or writers. That's why you should always get in with them. You see, what we chaps do may be all right in its little way but what really counts is the fact that if it weren't for

the existence of critics, we shouldn't be around at all or would just be on the dole or running chicken farms. Never make cheap jokes about critics. You've got to remember this: the critic is above criticism because he has the good sense never to do anything. He's up there helping us poor little guys to understand what the hell we're doing, which is a jolly helpful thing, you must agree. After all, who wants to read or listen to what some poor old writer has pumped out of his diseased heart when he can read a balanced and reasoned judgment about life, love and literature from an aloof and informed commentator. . . . .

MRS. JAMES: Do you see art as going in any particular direction now?

WYATT;   I can hardly see the table in front of me. All art is simply criticism now. Posturing as art, self-evaluation, categorising, constitutional, branded, hectoring and elbowing everyone out of the way.'[43]

In spite of that fact that Wyatt, in that extract, sounds rather like an elderly Jimmy Porter who has done nothing much but read the Sunday reviews throughout the whole span of time between *Look Back in Anger* and his retirement to a nameless sub-tropical island which is neither Africa nor Europe, there is much in it that is revealing. Osborne's 'critic' stands over against the writer because he is 'balanced', 'aloof' and 'informed': and because 'he has the good sense never to do anything' – i.e. to 'make' anything. The writer, by contrast, is the reverse of aloof: his work is 'pumped' out of his 'diseased heart'. It is achieved, that is, by the utmost exertion from a depth of 'felt' response to the 'sickness' of the artistic condition. Osborne's anger is for the critic who disregards the human *cost* of 'making', whose approach is wholly theoretical and intellectualised. Todorov's critic who never concerns himself with an actual text exactly indicates the kind of criticism under attack here:

> 'The nature of structural analysis will be essentially theoretical and non-descriptive; in other words, the aim of such a study will never be the description of a concrete work. The work will be considered as the manifestation of an abstract structure, merely out of its possible realisations.'[44]

The point at issue is that the writer is claiming an active relationship with some kind of 'felt' reality: the critic is rejecting the notion of any such 'reality' as relevant: for him there is only the theoretical reality of projected linguistic structures. Insofar as there is a refusal to engage with the writer's 'felt reality' the 'judgments' reached can be felt by the writer to be not only irrelevant but perverse, doctrinaire and diminishing.

Yet the critic is working within his own framework of 'reality'. What is required, clearly, is a notion of 'ultimates' large enough to accommodate both his own detached theoretical 'judgment' and the urgent 'felt' judgment of the creator-writer. Ionesco once pointed towards the possibility:

> 'The truth of fiction is more profound, more charged with meaning, than everyday reality. . . . (It takes) into account our basic truths and our fundamental obsessions: love, death, astonishment.'

The critic's act of 'judgment' needs to assert some kind of engagement with these 'basic truths'; but must do so in a context which looks beyond the writer to the structures within which he writes. Graham Hough has put this most cogently:

> 'At the higher level of abstraction formal theory is very simply stated: art has only one law, the proper perfection of the work itself. But each art has its own medium. That of literature is language; and language represents things, persons, actions,

emotions, and the structural relations between them. What can be the law of perfection for material so directly mimetic of the whole of human experience?'[45]

We must note in passing that Hough assumes the mimetic function of literature, and that he also argues from an implied stability both of reality and of relationship between a word and that which it signifies. As we have seen, all these are in question. Yet even if we reduce his comments to language within literary discourse, and the structural relations between those things which such language represents, his main demand remains unassailed. It is the demand for 'perfection', and the seeking out of what that law of 'perfection' might be.

It is here that the 'fictional' mimetic, 'content' view of literature and the aesthetically pleasing, 'form' view of literature can be seen as coming together. For Runquaya Hasan has noticed that where language 'calls attention it itself' by its forms, for what it is as language, rather than as a vehicle for information, such literary 'foregrounding' needs 'motivation' to explain it. Such motivation she finds in a 'unity' of topic or of theme which orders the patterning of the text without being explicit within it:

> 'So far as its own nature is concerned, the theme (or regulative principle) of a literary work may be seen as a generalisation or an abstraction. . . . A certain set of situations, a configuration of events, etc., is seen not only as itself (i.e. a particular happening) but also as a manifestation of some deep underlying principle.'[46]

This reference to 'deep underlying principles' takes one *beyond* language structures and yet gives them regulation or patterning. As such it unites the critical formularies. Nathan Scott, in an essay called 'The Vision in the Poetic Act', put it in this way:

> 'For although the literary work is a special sort of linguistic structure, that which holds the highest interest for us is the

special seizure of reality towards which this structure is instrumental.'[47]

This 'special seizure of reality' is, again, a function of words. Professor Clifford Leech in a lecture on Shakespeare once commented that the 'writer's task was to make alive the real': and D. J. Enwright has provided a gloss on this which leads us straight into the terms within which the critical task of judgment can be undertaken. He quoted Goethe as saying that, while the eye, 'the most facile of our organs of receptivity', may be thought of as the clearest of the senses, yet:

> 'The inner sense is still clearer, and to it *by means of words* belongs the most sensitive and clear receptivity. (There is) no true substitute for that inner sense or the words which activate it: which is why the poems of Wilfred Owen and Isaac Rosenberg still convey the experience of trench warfare more cogently, more enduringly, than the most powerful documentary film.'[48]

We are back to our study of 'words' and 'Word' again, this time providing a context in which the critic's proper task of 'judging' can level with the artist's creative seizure of reality. How a Logos theology helps us in this we shall discuss in the next chapter.

There are obviously important implications for both critic and writer in a grounding of criticism in theology in the way suggested. I have tried to show so far how far a theology of creation may be seen to relate to a human model of making; and how current critical dissensions raise serious problems of critical 'base', to which such a creation theology has something relevant to offer. It is necessary now to go further, to discover what patterns might emerge from all this in both creative 'making' and in critical judgment.

CHAPTER FIVE

Some conclusions

We come now to consider what might be some of the implications of the various lines of thought we have been examining
in the foregoing pages. What insights can we gain theologically
from the ferment we have confronted in literary criticism, and
the patterns we have perceived in 'making', divine and human? And what can theology offer as solvent for the dilemma
and disarray of the critics?

I want to propose in this chapter two main concepts. One
has to do with what, for reasons which I hope will become
clear, I will call the 'technique' of the Gospel. The other has
to do with what the theology of judgment has itself to say to
the critical enterprise. For both, 'word', 'Logos', is an essential component, in the context of a Trinitarian theology.

The Gospel and the language of imagery.
We may begin, usefully, with E. L. Mascall, publishing his
Theology and the Gospel of Christ in 1978, at the very moment
when *The Myth of God Incarnate* became, on its first appear-
ance, the subject of immediate and violent debate. Professor
Mascall added an appendix (directed against the latter book)
to give force and thrust to his thesis. The main urgency of his
argument was that theologians had lost their way because they
tried to explain and analyse, to define conceptually, instead
of responding to the language of *image* which is the Gospel's,
that language of poetic 'making' which is resistant to logical

summary.[1] George Steiner had already noted precisely the same danger for the critics of a literary text:

> 'The issue is straightforward but needs exact phrasing. The analytic modes which we can focus on a text are numerous and fairly well defined.
>
> They include the bibliographical, the philosophical, the historical, the psychological, the sociological, the biographic, and several more. Let us suppose that we have brought each of these "readings" to bear, that there is no linguistic, formal contextual aspect. . . . to which we have not applied the relevant discipline of elucidation. Yet invariably the sum of our understanding will fall short of the facts of meaning before us. If it were otherwise, our exegesis would produce an active tautology, a counterpart. . . . which would in every respect of significance be the equal of the original.'[2]

Such, equally, is the difficulty of 'reading' the Gospel if Mascall is correct in viewing the faith as essentially communicated by means of the language of images, rather than by means of argument. It is a view strongly affirmed by many, perhaps none more clearly than R. E. C. Browne in his *The Ministry of The Word*:

> 'The Christian religion can never be presented without imagery. Exact prose could not replace the allusiveness that makes imagery the only precision in proclaiming the Gospel. What could be used to illuminate the Passion other than the imagery of the broken bread, the thirty silver coins, the roar of the crowd, the scourge, the crown of thorns, the Cross and the empty tomb at dawn?. . . . In the high matters of life a man does not search for truth, he waits expectantly for it; it finds him and he gazes at it. Thus in religion contemplation is a more characteristic activity than analysis. . . .'[3]

It is obviously impossible in a study of this kind to embark on a full examination of the nature of the language of imagery as a vehicle of the Gospel. It is not only that the topic is a wide, profound and intricate one, already well documented. It is that the very nature of 'the Gospel' is in itself *in one sense* metaphorical, a glimpse through similitude into the nature of God, since it is not to be supposed that his dealings with man exhaust the fullness of his nature. This is, of course, *in no sense* to reject the historicity of the Incarnation. Quite the reverse: it is to root God's intervention in space and time as a material and active metaphor for that which is beyond space and time.

As aspects of this we might consider how Christ himself is recorded as using the language of similitude: 'the Kingdom of God is like. . . .'; 'to whom then shall I liken you?' And further, how the metaphorical mode (in very different forms) is used as variously as, for instance, in the very different theologies of the Epistle to the Hebrews, the First Epistle of Peter, and the Gospel of John. From the exposition of the nature of the young Church to the great 'I' discourses in John it is 'image' which suggests and controls our understanding. 'You are a royal priesthood, a holy nation'[4]; 'you are not come to. . . . a blazing fire, and darkness and gloom and a tempest and the sound of a trumpet. . . . but to Mount Zion and to the city of the living God'[5]; 'I am the Bread of life'[6]; 'I am the true vine'[7]; 'I am the Way'[8]. The great metaphors forever invite interpretation and exegesis, but defy rationalisation.

The cumulative effect of this mode is to be seen, rather engagingly, in John Bunyan's riposte in the face of his Puritan brethren's strong criticism, when he defended his own use of image, similitude, in *The Pilgrim's Progress*, declaring in his verse preface that his method has the best validation, that of God's own use:

'But must I needs want solidness, because
By metaphors I speak? Were not God's laws,
His gospel laws, in olden times held forth
By shadows, types, and metaphors? Yet loath
Will any sober man be to find fault
With them, lest he be found for to assault

The Highest Wisdom. No; he rather stoops,
And seeks to find out what by pins and loops,
By calves and sheep, by heifers and by rams,
By birds and herbs, and by the blood of lambs,
God speaketh to him; and happy is he
That finds the light and grace that in them be.'[9]

Of course, more deeply than the *instances* given there is a sense in which the Incarnation itself must be understood as a dramatic metaphor, an active similitude. It does not only reveal God in action, it asserts a quality. 'This is what God does' is correlate with "this is what he is like'. The role of similitude is made quite explicit: 'He who has seen me has seen the Father'[10]; 'the very stamp of his nature' (or, as the Authorised Version puts it, 'the express image of his person').[11]

Metaphor and metonymy.
Yet if there can be no doubt that theologically speaking Christ as the metaphor of God opens up for us perceptions of and responses to the very nature and activity of God, there is more yet to be understood. For if we distance ourselves from this mode of knowing God sufficiently to ask what we mean, *in the context of literary criticism*, by using the term 'metaphor', of Christ, some interesting possibilities arise from the current debate, which have potential theological implications. I can merely indicate them here: it would be for others to pursue and develop them more fully.

These possibilities arise from some of the work of the 'structuralists' or 'new formalists', when seen in the light of the 'Logos' model of creation we looked at in chapter three. Throughout this study I have tried to indicate those aspects of structuralism that seem to me fruitful in the inquiries they raise, while rejecting the ideology (or lack of it) behind the inquiries. One of the more fruitful explorations arising out of this 'new formalism' seems to me that of David Lodge's analysis of metaphor and metonymy, based on Jakobson's perceptions of language use.[12]

David Lodge bases his own exposition of the 'technique' of metaphor, how it works, what it *is*, on Jakobson's theory of language use, as expounded (though in highly condensed form) in 'Two Aspects of Language and Two Types of Aphasic Disturbances' first published in *Fundamentals of Language* (1956) by Jakobson and Morris Halle. In it he gives the grounds for and implications of the view that there are two characterising structures of formal language: that of association by contiguity, of coherence within a single world of discourse, which he calls 'metonymy'; and that of association by comparison, joining a plurality of worlds. To this he gives the label, 'metaphor'. This distinction becomes of far-reaching significance when the linguistic basis for these two structures becomes clear.

'Selection' and 'combination'.

Jakobson, in working on language disorders, used Saussure's basic principle that language itself has a twofold character, in that its use involves two operations – selection and combination. To speak or write, one selects certain 'linguistic entities' and combines them into 'linguistic units of a higher complexity'. But certain laws govern the selection, and control the combination. Neither is haphazard, or the result would be gibberish. The *'selection'* must be made from all the terms available which are 'like' in having the appropriate identical kernel of meaning but are disparate in other ways. The *'combination'* must be made by juxtaposing those items selected, in a coherence.

For instance, let us take the analogy of clothing. A man dressing for the day ahead must 'select' from all the hats available, from all the jackets available, from all the trousers, and from all the shoes. Hat, jacket, trousers and shoes are the 'kernels' of meaning, that which is 'like'. Consider now a man who chooses a bowler hat, pinstripe jacket, pinstripe trousers, highly polished black shoes for going to work in the morning.

On returning home he changes into tweed cap, tweed jacket, sports trousers, and walking shoes. 'The 'hat' and the 'cap' are 'like' in that – of different worlds – they have the same 'meaning' or function. They 'cover' the same area. Similarly the two jackets, and the trousers and shoes. Each proclaims 'selection' out of the infinite world of hats, of jackets, of trousers, of shoes.

Now, in putting together the first group of clothes our man was 'combining' these units in a coherence which gave a 'message', was a kind of sentence. If he had worn the walking shoes and the cap with his pinstripe jacket and trousers he would have shown a defective sense of 'combination'. There would have been a disjunction in the message, an error in the tone (though not the grammar) of the sentence.

Similarly, if he had put the jacket on his legs and the shoes on his hands, our man would have indicated that he was defective in the principle of selection – that he did not understand what made for similitude: that all jackets 'covered' the body, shoes the feet, and so on. The units of the 'sentence' would be distorted – an adverb where a noun was needed, or a pronoun used instead of a verb. The very 'categories' would be forced.

Jakobson had noted that aphasia (severe speech disability) could be located not only under the traditional sending and receiving of a verbal message, but more fundamentally in the distortion of or deficiency in either the selection or the combination axis of language, or both. Someone suffering from 'selection deficiency' could only speak in a clear context. He needed an actual situation to sustain discourse, unable to perceive 'category' or 'likeness' without the concrete 'visual aid' or 'context' before him. Disorder in the 'combination' axis resulted in chaotic word order, or the disappearance of all connectives. In such case, 'likeness' could be perceived, but coherent combination of categories or 'likes' was not possible.

Lodge, following Jakobson, argues that metaphor and metonymy are polar opposites in the structures of language use corresponding to the selection and combination axes of language. When a metaphor is used, or the metaphorical mode is employed, the writer is identifying essential similarities between what are otherwise different worlds. He is bringing together the disparate to indicate the essential similitude. When metonymy is used (its usual definition is that of using the 'part' or 'adjunct' as a symbol for the whole, e.g. 'sceptre' for 'authority') the writer is recognising relationship and co-herence within a single world: he is emphasising – often by paring away the obvious or trite – the contiguous, that which exists in observable and realistic relationship with the other.

Metonymy has often been seen as an adjunct or part of the metaphorical mode, and in its more immediate impact that would seem to be the case – the 'sceptre' is a substitution for the concept 'authority', a selected 'image' to stand for the whole. But more fundamentally what is being observed here is that the ability in language to select within a category is different at base, even opposed to, recognising how those selected units of many categories may be combined coherently into a message. And so too the perception of similitude – of the genuinely 'like' – in spite of vast disparities, is different from the perception of what coheres, what is consonant, what is the proper and natural adjunct within an overall pattern. Lodge points out, for instance, that the 'realistic' novel is largely metonymic while drama is largely metaphorical. Epic poetry is metonymic and lyrical metaphoric; and so on.

'Metaphor' and 'metonymy' in the parables.

It would be a fruitful exercise to apply this understanding to the parables of Jesus and see how they offered new wealth when opened up in this way. One might perhaps just note as an example that the parable of the Prodigal Son takes on an extra dimension thus: we begin to perceive how it functions, how it speaks to our hearts.[13] For its mode almost throughout is metonymic: a coherent picture is built up of a realistic family grouping, father, older son, younger son, against a background which is 'realistic', coherent within its culture in wealth, status, property management. The father is well dressed – rings, best robes; the property is rich – it survives the paying out to the younger son, it supports in reasonable comfort – 'bread enough and to spare' – a number of servants; its wealth includes the goats which are the index of wealth of the day. The property is 'placed': there is a road leading to it which figures in the story, and it has a wide view – it commands perspective 'a great way off'. All these are contiguous detail, adjunct to each other to build a coherent and realistic picture, identifiable pieces of a whole to outline something that is instantly recognisable.

But it is the use of the metapohoric mode in conjunction with this metonymy which speaks to our hearts. For balancing this recognisable and reproducible picture is that of the kingdom of heaven. What is it 'like'? Like the father who in this context of coherence appropriates another dimension: 'For this my son was dead and is alive again; he was lost and is found'. Nothing realistic or contiguous here. It grows out of the elemental and profound patterns of life and death, loss and recovery, whose 'like' is to be found in cultural pictures and scenes very different from, not consonant with, the one described. And behind them Jesus suggests, in this 'similitude' which brings together different worlds, a 'likeness' which transcends not only the disparate human social worlds, but the disparity between the Kingdom of God and the kingdoms of this world. The metaphor is of divine forgiveness, and its crossing with the metonymy in the story suggests its dynamic power and startling implications for the human race.

Christ the 'Metaphor' of God.

But perhaps more profoundly even than the implications for our reading of the parables is the fresh understanding we can gain of what it means to speak of Christ as a 'metaphor' of God. The metonymy of destruction and dereliction is built up powerfully for us in the events between Palm Sunday and Good Friday: but when we see him on the Cross as the metaphor of God we begin to conceive how a coherent world picture, detail by detail, has been cut across by the conjunction of disparate worlds, the divine and human, at the point where similitude is total. This is God, on the Cross, in precisely the same sense that Jesus was the Way or the Light or the True Vine. A 'plurality of worlds' is joined, each interpreted in terms of the other. The metaphoric mode of the Gospel here totally alters the cumulative effect of that coherent and suffocating metonymic world of plotters whispering, thirty pieces of silver, armed guard at night, law court, splintering wood of the Cross, and agonising fleshly pain.

There is of course much more. The 'metaphor' of God here displayed is of a man condemned as criminal, a social reject, a failure, whose wandering life had led to collision with authority and an early and disgraceful death. As such the 'similitude' draws into oneness, not only the Father and the Son, but *therefore* the Father and the abandoned, derelict and disgraced of humanity. It is not only the 'worthy poor' who are 'metaphored' on the Cross, but the disgraced and disgusting, the unattractive and repellant, who in the metonymy of the world are beyond hope.

Jurgen Moltmann's magnificent central chapter in *The Crucified God* included in its closing paragraphs what amounts to a statement of this coming together in similitude of disparate worlds:

'. . . The godforsaken and rejected man can accept himself when he comes to know the crucified God who is with him and has already accepted him. If God has taken upon himself death on the cross, he has also taken upon himself all of life and real life, as it stands under death, law and guilt. In so doing he makes it possible to accept life whole and entire and death whole and entire. Man is taken up, without limits and conditions, into the life and suffering, the death and resurrection of God, and in faith participates corporeally in the fullness of God.'[14]

God the 'perfect Word'.

Then again, theologically speaking, it seems to me that there is in this metaphoric/metonymic approach scope for a deeper understanding of that 'Logos' model we looked at earlier. Steiner reminds us that Mallarmé spoke of the fulfilment of the universe, of all creation, being 'Le Livre', 'book' or 'word' so perfected that it subsumed in itself all that ever was or would be. The 'Logos' language can carry this – 'all things were made through him'[15] and 'the fullness of him who fills all in all'.[16] But if we begin to ask what is the sense of this to us, we find ourselves clutching at imponderables.

It is here that the analysis of all word use as basically of two modes, selection and combination, metaphor and metonymy, aids us.

For God as 'perfect word' can be understood in both modes, disjunct in neither, harmoniously balanced in the two. Neither, that is, is dominant; unlike all, even the best, of our art. What might this mean? It would follow, I think, that in his address to creation the categories of making and loving ('creation' and 'redemption') are sustained between the human and divine worlds, points of similitude between the disparate; while what he 'says' in the natural world will cohere with what he 'says' in his acts and in his people: the combination will cohere. More: on the metaphoric axis we are led to perceive the infinities of God's love: on the metonymic axis we are led to ponder the time/space contiguity of God's love. There is enough here, I think, to suggest how the *critical* approach may open up the *theological*.

'Story' as a function of divine metaphor.

We might note a corollary to this, in the wake of the debate of the last few years concerning the nature of 'story' and its role in the Gospel. I propose here, for the sake of the argument, a view of 'story' (only one of many possible views) as a function of metaphor, a kind of sustained narrative image. In such terms the life, death and resurrection of Jesus can be seen as *itself a living parable*, or 'story of God', told *by* him and *of* him. As a parable it can be seen to be self-coherent in all contiguous detail, yet spanning different worlds by its 'likeness'.

We may remind ourselves of some aspects of creative 'making' (which would be applicable to 'story') that we identified in chapter three: paradox; self-emptying in the outpouring of self for others; 'judgment' – i.e. true perception; and that 'redeeming' which is the transforming of the spoilt or maimed into glory or 'felicity'.[17] In 'the story of God', following this model, divine immanence would inhere in the story as its 'object' and divine transcendence as its narrator or 'subject'. (we might note here that arguments have been put forward for a 'narrative' grammar as fundamental as those linguistic principles identified within semiotics.[18]) It is here we begin to see a way through the difficult question of how Christ can be both Creator and created, noted above in chapter three as a crucial problem in considering the activity of God the Maker as a ground for human making.[19] 'Story' suggests how 'outpouring' can create a life and yet remain undiminished; a costly 'giving' in which the story-teller is forgotten behind the story he tells and yet in which his nature is stamped on what he has created, indeed is expressed by it.

The 'readerly' and the 'writerly'.

Moreover, in the sense that the concept of 'reader-power' has some validity (as we saw in chapter four[20]) the story 'belongs' also to us as 'listeners' or 'readers' – or as the Gospel puts it, 'hearers of the word'. For in perceiving it we respond to it, even at the human level of 'story', by sharing its creativity:

'It is the conjoint effort of author and reader which brings upon the scene that concrete and imaginary object which is the work of the mind.[21]

Again there is help for us in a suggestion from the new formalists. Richard Miller has identified for us (following

Barthes) two kinds of 'story' or 'text': the 'readerly' (*lisible*) and the 'writerly' (*scriptible*).[22] The first is orderly and logical, it is to be consumed passively, it does not force us as readers to creative engagement; as readers we 'follow' it. The second makes us not only consumers 'but producers, because we write ourselves into it, we construct meaning for it as we read it, and ideally these meanings are infinitely plural.'[23]

Again we abandon the posited ideological basis for this (that plurality of meanings is possible because there is no 'truth') for the Christian basis that the 'truth of God' is broad enough to contain a diversity of valid readings. What is more germane here is the insight into how we, contemporary readers, enter into or apprehend Jesus, the 'story of God', within both the historic/cultural and the eternal frameworks. Trinitarian theology suggests a viable process for this act of 'reading'. The accounts of the activity of the Holy Spirit both as foretold by Christ and as recorded within Acts suggests that it is the Spirit who 'reads' Jesus the story of God within us and in-volves us in a 'writerly' response. Hence the truth of Gustav Aulen's statement that all humanity is caught up on the drama of salvation, choice and refusal. It is an aspect of 'metaphor' which bears much further reflection.

The stimulus to prophetic judgment.

It is this Trinitarian theology which leads us to the second main concept I want to look at in this chapter, that of what a theology of judgment has to say to the critical enterprise. That it not only has something to say, but is under necessity of its very nature to say it, has been well observed by Professor John Heywood Thomas:

'Theology must be concerned with culture because it is not merely concerned with some isolated event but with the historical event of Jesus Christ. A Christian theology is a theology of creation as much as a theology of redemption. . . . .If we are able to argue that there is a continued presence of the Triune God in his world then culture can equally be

criticised by appeal to this norm. The confession that we have
the mind of Christ is not only the revelation of the world's
sacramental quality: it is the stimulus to prophetic judgment.'[24]

It is this 'stimulus to prophetic judgment' we need now to
examine. We noted in chapter three that 'creation, judgment
and redemption' were the traditional heads under which
Christians spoke of God's dealings with the world, and we
examined something of what this meant. At that point it was
important to recognise that 'judgment' – the activity of right
discernment – was an important and necessary element of
human 'making' grounded in the nature and activity of God.
'Judgment', that is, was axial: it was that just discerning of
creation which led properly to its redeeming and transforming, by re-creation, into a 'new creation'. And in our examination of the critical enterprise we noted that 'judgment' was
an inevitable aspect of it. But our contemporary culture con-
fuses us on the *meaning* of 'judgment'. How are we to understand it?

We may turn to some words of Christ attributed in St.
John's Gospel:

'For judgment I came into this world, that those who do not
see may see, and that those who see may become blind.'[25]

and again,

'He who rejects me and does not receive my sayings has a
judge; the word that I have spoken will be his judge on the last
day.'[26]

and finally,

'And this is the judgment, that the light has come into the
world, and men loved darkness rather than light, because their
deeds were evil.'[27]

I quote these simply as instances of the very strong biblical affirmation that Christ's Incarnation is *in itself* to be seen (or felt) as judgment: because it reveals distortion in men's vision, because it elicits a response which reveals the heart, and because *in its quality* it is 'of', 'related to' the Last Day. They are 'like': that is – it cuts across the metonymy of space and time with the metaphoric linking of the worlds 'beyond time', because it is in essence '*like*' those worlds – at one with them. One of the most helpful ways, that is, of understanding something of the nature of 'judgment' and the sense in which it is one with salvation is by entering into its meaning through the 'metaphoric' mode of the Incarnation, and in particular of the Crucifixion, in the sense I suggested earlier.

The Incarnation as Judgment.

In what particular sense may we say that the Crucifixion is a metaphor of 'judgment'? What is its action?

I have already quoted from Moltmann's chapter on the 'Crucified God' earlier in this chapter. I want to return to this because in its analysis it seems to me to indicate the true nature of the judgment Christ was to be understood as declaring. Moltmann writes:

> 'When God becomes man in Jesus of Nazareth, he not only enters into the finitude of man, but in his death on the cross also enters into the situation of man's godforsakeness. In Jesus he doesn't die the natural death of a finite being, but the violent death of the criminal on the cross, the death of complete abandonment by God. The suffering in the person of Jesus is abandonment, rejection, by God, his Father. . . . God does not become a law, so that men participate in him through obedience to a law. . . . He humbles himself and takes upon himself the eternal death of the godless and the godforsaken, so that all the godless and the godforsaken can experience communion with him.'[28]

What may we infer about the nature of 'judgment' from this? If there is something of the very essence, something 'like' – or 'alike' – in this and in the Last Day, it is not immediately easy to see. The *Revelation of St. John the Divine* suggests a Last Day whose form, at least is quite different in the authority with which condemnation and approval are apportioned and enacted in eternal effect: and the parable of the judgment enunciated by our Lord uses the same frame work.[29] So in what sense is Jesus's 'word' (not *words*) from the Cross to be understood as a 'judgment', at 'the Last Day'?

The theology of creation we have examined is our clue, for at the nub of this creation theory was the concept that the 'creating' gift of the Creator was the 'giving of giving', the giving, that is, to his creatures of the ability to give, the potential for self-emptying. This would indeed show the Crucifixion as opening up, offering, the very nature and basis of 'judgment':

> 'The Son suffers in his love being forsaken by the Father as he dies. The Father suffers in his love the grief of the death of the Son. In that case, whatever proceeds from the event between the Father and the Son must be understood as the spirit of surrender of the Father and the Son, as the spirit which creates love for forsaken men, as the spirit which brings the dead alive.'[30]

The 'Spirit', therefore, proceeding from the event of the Cross, creates in the 'godforsaken', those on whom 'judgment' is due, the possibility and the force of new life. For if life is to be re-created, purged and renewed, its distortions have to be exposed, lifted up to scrutiny, by that which not only enacts the exposure but itself suffers the guilt and misery of the distortion and corrects it.

It is this which lies behind Karl Barth's marvellous exposition of the Last Judgment. He invites us to repudiate the apocalyptic horrors of Michaelangelo's conception since 'how these damned folk sink in the pool of hell' is 'certainly not the point'.[31] Question 52 of the Heidelberg Catechism asks: 'What comfort hast thou by the coming again of Christ to judge the quick and the dead?' Answer: 'That in all my

miseries and persecution *I look with my head erect* for the very
same, who before yielded Himself unto the judgment of God
for me and took away all malediction from me, to come Judge
from heaven.' Judgment, that is, is good news, tidings of joy.
'With head erect' the new-made creature confronts his future,
for the Judge who comes is he who previously offered himself
to accept and *take to himself* the right discernment, the just
and loving gaze of God, and its consequences. The ancient
and lovely Collect for Christmas Eve sums it up:

> 'O God, who makest us glad with the yearly remembrance of
> the birth of thy only Son, Jesus Christ: Grant that as we
> joyfully receive him for our redeemer, so we may with sure
> confidence behold him, when he shall come to be our judge:
> who liveth and reigneth with thee and the Holy Spirit, one
> God, world without end.
>
> > Amen.'

For the activity of Justice is two-fold: a right discerning: a
setting right. Justice that does not compass both is not justice.
Hence its essential nature within 'making' as a part of creation
and resurrection. Hence, too, the wrongness of any criticism
which merely diminishes or destroys. Resurrection is the concomitant of judgment more surely, in the divine making of
things, than that death and damnation so popularly associated
with it.

> 'The Spirit is present in the whole creation, preparing for the
> final gathering up of all into Christ, the Son. He is present in
> the core of each being, in the heart of each man, as a ceaseless
> call and longing. . . . In him the elect already possess and enjoy
> the *things-to-come*, for all things to come are already present in
> the eternity of God, and he who possesses the Spirit possesses
> everything that belongs to the Father and the Son.'[32]

It is this final setting-in-order which we can see as the proper
basis for that 'putting right' which is the literary maker's
highest art. Barth reminds us that in the biblical world of

thought the judge is not primarily the one who rewards some and punishes others; he is the man who creates order and restores what has been destroyed. 'The Judge who puts some on the left and others on the right is in fact He who has yielded Himself to the judgment of God *for me* and has taken away all malediction from me.'[33]

Judgment may therefore be seen with creation and salvation as three aspects of one action. Indeed, Barth's gloss arises specifically from such a vision.

De-worded man.

I propose in conclusion to look at some immediate implications of this in our present context in this study. I spoke earlier of how there is a sense in which God is Mallarme's Le Livre, the 'perfect word'. In much the same sense it is possible to describe man's dereliction and loss in terms of 'de-wording'. His loss of articulacy is a powerful symbol of his condition. It is interesting, in this connection, to note that David Lodge in describing Jakobson's work on aphasia (severe speech disability) commented:

'If modern literature is exceptionally difficult to understand, this can only be because of some dislocation or distortion of either the selection or the combination axes of language; and of some modern writing, e.g. the work of Gertrude Stein and Samuel Beckett, it is not an exaggeration to say that it aspires to the condition of aphasia.'[34]

This de-wording of man as figurative of his condition has been well traced by Steiner, who identifies four aspects of it. He points to Dada's demand for 'an end to the word' as nihilistic as well as aesthetic; to the work of logical positivism, of Wittgenstein, and modern philosophers from Moore to Austin and Quine, whose stirring of doubt has 'made language look messier, more fragile'; he notes that the enormous expansion of exact sciences has involved passing 'into the keeping of the non-verbal semantic systems of mathematics. . . an ever-increasing portion of sensory and conceptual reality'. And finally he reminds us of the 'cheapening, the dehumanisation, the muddling of words through the mass media and through the lies of barbarism in modern politics', which – for instance – George Orwell had earlier investigated.[35] Today, Steiner comments, Pisarev's slogan 'a pair of boots outweighs Shakespeare and Pushkin', has come into its own.

A powerful expression of this 'de-wording' appears in the play *West of Suez*, by John Osborne (from which I quoted earlier in this book) when the character Jed, a 'drop-out' who has lounged offensively but silently in and out of the play throughout its length, suddenly, immediately prior to the murder of the central figure who is a writer, turns on him in a torrent of obscenity and proclaims the death of words. Words 'is going to be the first to go':

'. . . . One person, not like any one of your here, even if he's the God-damnest cretin, I'd make him God, yes, man, rather than you. You hear? Hear me. Listen to me if you can hear anything but the sound of your own selves and present. I'm not interested in your arguments, not that they are, of your so-called memories. . . . The only thing that matters, man, is blood, man. Blood. . . . You know what that means? No, no, you surely as to hell don't. No, no, when you pigs, you pigs go. . . . All I see, and I laugh when I see it, man, I laugh, is you pigs barbecued. . . We're, yes, we're going to take over and don't you begin to forget it. Man, I feel real sorry for you lot. No, I don't. . . . of the theatre of the mind, baby, old moulding babies, except you won't. We count and we do, not like you, we really, really, do. . . . Why, we fall about laughing at you people, not people, you're not people, you pigs. We are people. We are. But not you. You don't understand and why should you because, believe me, babies, old failing babies, words, yes I mean words, even what I'm saying to you now, is going to be the first to go. Go, baby. Go.'[36]

This differs from Beckett's 'aspiration to aphasia' in its dominant note of aggression rather than mourning: but the condition is the same.

The metaphor of Babel.

One is reminded, in surveying this horrible and powerful sign of man's condition, of the correlate biblical sign:

'Now the whole earth had one language and few words. And as men migrated from the east, they found a plain in the land of Shinar and settled there. And they said to one another, "Come, let us make bricks, and burn them thoroughly." And they had brick for stone, and bitumen for mortar. Then they said, "Come, let us build ourselves a city, and a tower with its top in the heavens, and let us make a name for ourselves, lest we be scattered abroad upon the face of the whole earth." And the Lord came down to see the city and the tower, which the sons of men had built. And the Lord said, "Behold, they are one people, and they have all one language; and this is only the beginning of what they will do; and nothing that they propose to do will now be impossible for them. Come, let us go down, and there confuse their language, that they may not understand one another's speech." So the Lord scattered them abroad from there over the face of all the earth, and they left off building the city. Therefore its name was called Babel, because there the Lord confused the language of all the earth; and from there the Lord scattered them abroad over the face of all the earth.'[37]

There is a real sense in which this Genesis account of the first *diaspora* is, in Professor Heywood Thomas's words, a 'prophetic judgment'. Certainly it has ongoing, even gathering, vitality as an account of our own 'de-worded' state. (The details of frantic societal urge and armament stock-piling are, for instance, familiar and recognisable.) Most profoundly, what we know in it to be our condition is the frustration of non-communication, of scattering, of speech reduced to gibberish, of dispersion and division.

And it is here we perceive that the redemptive act of God engages our condition. For the Holy Spirit, he who 'proceeds from the Father and the Son', who in the words of Moltmann 'proceeds from the event between Father and Son on the Cross', is by virtue of that origin the spirit of surrender, the spirit who creates love for forsaken men, the spirit who brings the dead alive. This Spirit, in descending upon men at Pentecost, is signified as unifying and making communicative, bringing together at last the diaspora. Thus men, empowered with new life, 're-created', are described in Acts as discovering that their 'word' has been restored to them. This is the powerful symbol as St. Luke presents it of new life in Christ, the sign of man's healing and re-creation: that the power of the word is again his.

'When the day of Pentecost had come, they were all together in one place. And suddenly a sound came from heaven like the rush of a mighty wind, and it filled all the house where they were sitting. And there appeared to them tongues as of fire, distributed and resting on each one of them. And they were all filled with the Holy Spirit and began to speak in other tongues, as the Spirit gave them utterance.

Now there were dwelling in Jerusalem Jews, devout men from every nation under heaven. And at this sound the multitude came together, and they were bewildered, because each one heard them speaking in his own language. And they were amazed and wondered, saying, "Are not all these who are speaking Galileans? And how is it that we hear, each of us in his own native language? Parthians and Medes and Elamites and residents of Mesopotamia, Judea and Cappadocia, Pontus and Asia, Phyrgia and Pamphyllia, Egypt and the parts of Libya belonging to Cyrene, and visitors from Rome, both Jews and proselytes, Cretans and Arabians, we hear them telling in our own tongues the mighty works of God.' And all were amazed and perplexed, saying to one another, "What does this mean?" But others mocking said, "They are filled with new wine." '[38]

Fanfare for the makers.

So creation, judgment and redemption are here again seen as three aspects of Trinitarian activity. For man the maker (the writer and also his critic, the reader) the Trinitarian activity is the ground of his own. We may perhaps allow the final statement of this to modern writers, with whose current dilemma we began.

At the end of her most enriching selection of poems for *The New Oxford Book of English Verse* (1972), Dame Helen Gardner has placed as a single poem under her own title 'Epilogue', a short selection from Louis MacNeice's 'Autumn Sequel', which she entitles 'A Fanfare for the Makers':[39]

'A cloud of witnesses. To Whom? To what?
To the small fire that never leaves the sky.
To the great fire that boils the daily pot.

To all the things we are not remembered by,
Which we remember and bless. To all the things
That will not even notice when we die.

Yet lend the passing moment words and wings.

So Fanfare for the Makers: who compose
A book of words or deeds who runs may write
As many do who run, as a family grows

At times like sunflowers turning towards the light,
As sometimes in the blackout and the raids
One joke composed an island in the night,

As sometimes one man's kindliness pervades
A room or house or village, as sometimes
Merely to tighten screws or sharpen blades

Can match a meaning, as to hear the chimes
At midnight means to share them, as one man
In old age plants an avenue of limes

And before they bloom can smell them, before they span
The road can walk beneath the perfected arch,
The merest green print when the lives began

Of those who walk there with him, as in default
Of coffee men grind acorns, as in despite
Of all assaults conscripts counterassault.

As mothers sit up late night after night
Moulding a life, as miners day by day

114

Descend blind shafts, as a boy may flaunt his kite

In an empty nonchalant sky, as anglers play
Their fish, as workers work and can take pride
In spending sweat before they draw their pay,

As horsemen fashion horses while they ride,
As climbers climb a peak because it is there,
As life can be confirmed even in suicide:

To make is such. Let us make. And set the weather fair.'

Presumably Dame Helen placed this 'Fanfare for the Makers' as a final comment on the 'making' of the poets represented in the book. Their work witnesses to that energy, light and heat which maintain our life, and the things which raise in us a sense of blessing. But what goes into the 'making' is *creation:*

'who compose
A book of words or deeds who runs may write
As many who run'

and *judgment*:

'As sometimes
Merely to tighten screws or sharpen blades
Can catch a meaning'

and *redemption*:

'As sometimes in the blackout and the raids
One joke composed an island in the night,
As sometimes one man's kindliness pervades
A room or house or village'

Louis MacNeice, a modern, though not contemporary, writer, is explicitly not a Christian. Yet what he has observed in the laws of human 'making' are energies and patterns which correspond to the divine making, and which are gathered up

together in that final act of the created order, that last affirmation of the divine 'making' envisaged in Revelation as the
last judgment. In it the operation of creation, judgment and
redemption come together, and the final making is one of
glory: since 'no part of created things and no moment of
created time lies outside the power of the Spirit, who is Lord,
to change from glory into glory.'[40] It is a glory that is reflected
in every little 'making' in which the world of space and time
allows us to delight. And since this is so, we can with Mac-
Neice, finally make the affirmation:

'To make is such. Let us make. And set the weather fair.'

Notes

Chapter One
1. O.U.P., 1959.
2. op cit., 'The Drunkenness of Noah', p. 79.
3. First section, lectures given in 1953: second section, lectures given in 1956.
4. M. H. Abrams, *The Mirror and the Lamp*, chapter 1, 1953.
5. Roland Barthes, 'Criticism as Language', *The Critical Moment*, 1964, reprinted in David Lodge, ed. *Twentieth Century Literary Criticism* 1972, pp. 650 following.
6. Eugenio Donato, 'The Two Languages of Criticism', *The Structuralist Controversy*, pp. 95, 96.
7. See pp. 74, 75 below.
8. Eugenio Donato, 'Of Structuralism and Literature', *Modern Language Notes*, LXXXII, 1967, p. 57.
9. David Lodge, *The Modes of Modern Writing*, Arnold, 1977, p. 65.
10. ibid. p. 62.
11. Catherine Belsey, *Critical Practice*, Methuen, 1980, p. 29.
12. Ibid., p. 5.
13. Helen Gardner, loc. cit., p. 21.
14. Saul Bellow, 'The Gonzaego Manuscripts', *Mosby's Memoirs and Other Stories*, Widenfeld and Nicolson, 1969.
15. Wallace Stevens, 'Two or Three Ideas', *Opus Posthumous*, ed. S. M. Morse, New York, 1957, pp. 206–9.
16. Alexander Solzhenitsyn, *One Word of Truth*, Bodley Head, 1972, p. 14 (for Nobel Speech 1970).
17. Leland Ryken, *Triumphs of the Imagination*, IVP, 1979, p. 234.
18. See particularly *Religion and Literature*, Oxford, 1971, and *The Interpretation of Otherness, Essays on Literature, Religion and Critical Method*, O.U.P. and New York, 1979.
19. An Order for Holy Communion, Series 3, 1971, Nicene Creed, p. 13

(cf. 'One God. . . . Maker of Heaven and earth, And of all things visible and invisible:' *The Book of Common Prayer* 1662).
20. See below, chapter four.

Chapter Two
 1. John Osborne, *West of Suez*, Faber, 1971, p. 73. Osborne is, of course, through his character Wyatt (no casual choice of name) quoting from W. B. Yeats (with, indeed, the whole symbolist debate lying within the phrase).
 2. Roland Barthes, 'To write an intransitive verb?', *The Structuralist Controversy*, ed. R. Macksey and E. Donato, Baltimore, 1972, p. 135.
 3. Published in *Ariel*, Faber, 1965.
 4. The words are 'objects' – i.e. the only objective reality discernible – in the symbolist sense: but this reality, itself the only one available to the poet, is a diminishing and transient one, since it resides only in the instant of use.
 5. Denis Donoghue, 'The Word within a Word', in *'The Waste Land' in Different Voices*, ed. A. D. Moody, Arnold, 1974, pp. 189–190.
 6. Paul Van Buren, *The Edges of Language*, S.C.M., 1972, pp. 46, 47.
 7. W. M. Urban, quoted by Cleanth Brooks in *'The Heresy of Paraphrase'*, 1968, p. 163.
 8. Arnold Wesker, *Roots*, Penguin, 1974, pp. 88, 89.
 9. Doris Lessing, *The Memoirs of a Survivor*, Picador, 1976, p. 100.
10. C. B. Cox, Editorial, *The Critical Quarterly*, vol. 14, No. 1, Spring 1972, p. 4.
11. op cit., pp. 89, 90.
12. Catherine Belsey, *Critical Practice*, Methven, 1980, pp. 29–36.
13. See C. Bronte, 'Editor's Preface to New Edition of *Wuthering Heights*', 1850, pp. XIX–XIV, under pseudonym of Currer Bell.
14. John Osborne, *Luther*, Act III, Sc. 2.
15. See below, chapter five.
16. John Osborne, *Luther*, Act III, Sc. 2.
17. See Peter Hebblethwaite, 'Draining the marshes of Christian phraseology', *The Times*, 27th July, 1974: 'The serious question. . . is whether Christians are obliged, by the very nature of their faith, to use special language, or whether they can simply exploit the language generally available.' What happens if the language generally available falsifies or distorts the faith the Christian would express? (The 1979 discussion on the Alternative Services Book is relevant.)
18. Edward Albee, *Who's afraid of Virginia Woolf?'*
19. From *The Pilgrim's Regress*, Bk. VIII.
20. From the translation by Dorothy L. Sayers, Penguin reprint, 1971, vol. 3, *Paradise*, p. 347.

Notes

Chapter Three

1. Or 'Creator'. See liturgical variants: e.g. Book of Common Prayer 1662, or An Order for Holy Communion, Series 3, 1971, Nicene Creed, p. 13. Note also 'And in one Lord Jesus Christ . . . Being of one substance with the Father, By whom all things were made. . .' Nicene Creed, 1662. See also the *Alternative Services Book* as authorised by General Synod, 1979.

2. See above, chapter two.

3. Professor Barbour points out that ta panta in the phrase di' houta panta probably means both the 'new' creation as in 2 Corinthians 5:18, and the 'totality of things' as in Colossians 1:17, 20, and Ephesians 1:10, 23. (In 'Creation, Wisdom and Christ', *Creation, Christ and Culture*, ed. Richard W. A. McKinney, T. & T. Clark, 1976, p. 30.)

4. Barbour (ibid.) quotes Kramer, *Christ, Lord, Son of God*, London, 1966, pp. 84–90, on the use of these phrases in early Christian worship, and notes that 'the celebration of the blessings of salvation by means of such language was a second stage; *the appeal to the Lord's present power was primary.*'

5. 2 Corinthians 5:17, 18.

6. See below, particularly the comments by Smulders.

7. Hebrews 1:1–3.

8. See above, chapter two, pp. 27ff.

9. Gustav Aulen, *The Drama and The Symbols*, S.P.C.K., 1970, pp. 51, 52.

10. *Encyclopaedia of Theology*, ed. Karl Rahner, Burns and Oates, 1975, essay on 'Creation', Peter Smulders, pp. 313–319.

11. See J. Moltmann below, p. 51 for an interesting further development on these ideas.

12. See, for instance, the essays in the *Theological Dictionary of the New Testament*, ed. Gerhard Kittel, (translated G. W. Bromiley) Eerdmans, 1967, vol. IV, pp. 69–143.

13. op. cit., p. 75.

14. op. cit., p. 90.

15. op. cit., p. 93.

16. cf. Ezekiel, and also (particularly) Psalms 33, 147:15–18.

17. See Klein Knecht, ed. Kittel, op. cit., p. 91. 'From the very first the New Testament Logos concept is alien to Greek thought. But it later became the point of contact between Christian doctrine and Greek philosophy.'

18. First Epistle of John, chapter 1, vv. 1, 2a, 4 (with variant reading).

19. Alasdair Heron, 'Logos, Image, Son: Some Models and Paradigms in Early Christology', *Creation, Christ and Culture*, op. cit., p. 48.

Notes

20. For a penetrating study of this principle in biblical revelation see F. Kermode, *The Genesis of Secrecy*, Harvard, 1979.
21. R. S. Barbour, op. cit., p. 34.
22. R. S. Barbour, op. cit., p. 36.
23. Loc. cit., p. 36 (italics my own): see below, particularly pp.
24. See chapter 2 above.
25. Philip Wheelwright, 'Religion and Poetry', *Encyclopaedia of Poetry and Poetics*, ed. Preminger, Warke and Hardison, Princeton, 1965, p. 688.
26. G. K̇ ¹, op. cit., pp. 125, 131.
27. I· ∴ion to this we might note Barbour's contention that the creative ∴ivity of 'Wisdom' is to be understood as continuous and effective in the earthly ministry of Christ, in, amongst other things, his teaching and his telling of the parables. 'For he taught them as one who had authority and not as the scribes.'
28. loc. cit., p. 129.
29. In this connection the sense of 'power having gone out of him' which the evangelists record as Christ's experience when healing – see e.g. the healing of the woman with the issue of blood, Luke 8:43–48 and Mark 5:22–43.
30. R. S. Barbour, op. cit., p. 35.
31. Genesis chapter 1, vv. 4, 10b, 12b, 18b, 21b, 25b, 31b.
32. cf. The image of the potter, Jeremiah 18:1–12; and see chapter two above.
33. 2 Corinthians 6:2.
34. Gustav Aulen, op. cit., p. 52.
35. loc. cit. (Italics my own.)
36. J. Moltmann, 'Creation and Redemption', *Creation, Christ and Culture*, op. cit., p. 119.
37. Walter de la Mare
'Shadows', *Collected Poems*, Everyman
38. N. J. O'Donoghue, 'Creation and Participation', in *Creation, Christ and Culture*, op. cit., p. 143.
39. op. cit., p. 146.
40. T. S. Eliot, Choruses from 'The Rock', from *Collected Poems 1909–1962*, Faber & Faber, 1963.
41. J. Moltmann, *Theology and Joy*, S.C.M., 1973, p. 41.
42. See N. J. O'Donoghue, op. cit., p. 144. He points to the Thomist background to this argument: the assumption is that some concepts, creation/creativity among them, are inherently of such a nature that they can be applied, though in differing ways, to both the finite and the infinite.
43. Karl Barth, *Church Dogmatics*, 'Creation', vol. 3, pt. III, p. 102.
44. See below, pp. 65, 68 following, for the 'redemptive' role of the artist.

45. Karl Barth, loc. cit., pp. 298, 299.
46. David Jones, *Epoch and Artist*, Faber, 1959, p. 52.
47. Adapted by David Jones, loc. cit., p. 126, n., from G. Dix, *The Shape of the Liturgy*. (This seems to me to link with the inherent 'life' we looked at earlier.)
48. loc. cit., p. 120.
49. N. J. O'Donoghue, op. cit., p. 146.
50. op. cit., p. 160.
51. S. T. Coleridge, *Biographia Literaria*, chapter 13.
52. Genesis 1:31.
53. Helen Oppenheimer, Pastoral Theology Lectures, University of Durham, February 1974.
54. Jeremiah 15:16, 19. (Kittel comments on the profound theological understanding of 'The Word' expressed in the book of Jeremiah.)
55. Kittel, op. cit., p. 166.
56. Proverbs 8:30. I am indebted to David Jones for his pinpointing of this translation.
57. J. Moltmann, op. cit., pp. 42, 43.
58. T. S. Eliot, *The Use of Poetry and The Use of Criticism*, Faber & Faber, 1933, p. 106.
59. N. J. O'Donoghue, op. cit., *passim*.
60. Giles B. Gunn, 'Literature and its Relation to Religion', *Religion and Literature*, Oxford, 1971, p. 13.
61. loc. cit.
62. From W. H. Auden: 'In memory of W. B. Yeats', *Collected Shorter Poems 1927–1957*, Faber, reprint of 1977, p. 143.

Chapter Four
1. See above, chapter one, p. 3.
2. John Ruskin, quoted by Catherine Belsey, op. cit., p. 9.
3. John Bayley, 'Against a New Formalism', *The Word in the Desert*, Critical Quarterly 10th Anniversary number, ed. C. B. Cox and A. E. Dyson, 1968, pp. 66, 67. (Italics my own.)
4. David Lodge, op. cit., p. 62.
5. Roland Barthes, quoted Lodge, op. cit., p. 62.
6. M. V. Abrams, op. cit., p. 11.
7. Sir Philip Sidney, 'An Apologie for Poetry', *Elizabethan Critical Essays*, ed. G. Gregory Smith, London, 1904, p. 158.
8. Sir Philip Sidney, loc. cit., p. 159.
9. See, for instance, David Paul Funt, 'Newer Criticism and Revolution' Hudson Review XXII, 1969, pp. 81, 96, and John Ellis, 'Ideology and Subjectivity', *Working Papers in Cultural Studies 9*, Spring 1976, p. 205.
10. Northop Frye, *Anatomy of Criticism*, Princeton, 1957, quoted Belsey, op. cit. p. 28.

Notes

11. W. K. Wimsatt Jr., *The Verbal Icon: Studies in Meaning*, Methuen, 1946, p. 5.
12. Stanley Fish, *Self-Consuming Artefacts: The Experience of Seventeenth Century Literature*, Univ. of California, 1972, pp. 387, 388, quoted Belsey, op. cit., p. 32.
13. See above, chapter two.
14. M. V. Abrams, op. cit., p. 17.
15. M. V. Abrams, loc. cit., p. 20.
16. John Stuart Mill, *Early Essays by John Stuart Mill*, ed. J. W. M. Gibbs, London, 1897, pp. 208–209.
17. John Keats (to Reynolds, 9th April, 1818), *Letters*, ed. Maurice Buxton Forman, 3rd edn., New York, 1948, p. 131.
18. Thomas Carlyle, 'Jean Paul Friedrich Richter', 1827, Works, ed. H. D. Traill, London, 1905, XXVI, 20.
19. C. Belsey, loc. cit., p. 17.
20. loc. cit., p. 27. (My own italics.)
21. loc. cit., p. 29.
22. W. J. Slatoff, *With Respect to Readers: Dimensions of Literary Response*, Cornell, 1970, p. 112 and p. 35.
23. Belsey, loc. cit., p. 33.
24. George Steiner, 'Text and Context', *On Difficulty and Other Essays*, O.U.P., 1980, pp. 14–17.
25. David Lodge, *The Modes of Modern Writing*, Arnold, 1977, p. 70.
26. David Lodge, loc. cit., p. 70.
27. Northop Frye, op. cit., p. 438, quoted by Catherine Belsey, op. cit., p. 23.
28. Mark Schorer, 'Technique as Discovery', *Hudson Review*, 1948, reprinted David Lodge, ed., *Twentieth Century Literary Criticism*, Longmans, 1972, p. 387.
29. Roland Barthes, *Writing Degree Zero*, transl. Lavers & Smith, 1967, p. 66.
30. Roland Barthes, 'To Write: An Intransitive Verb?', *The Structuralist Controversy*, ed. Macksey & Donato, Baltimore, 1972, p. 135.
31. Ibid., p. 141.
32. David Lodge, op. cit., p. 61.
33. Eugenio Donato, 'The Two Languages of Criticism', *The Structuralist Controversy*, pp. 95, 96.
34. See Introduction.
35. Denis Donoghue, 'The Word within a Word', *'The Waste Land' in Different Voices*, ed. A. D. Moody, Arnold, 1974.
36. T. S. Eliot, *Knowledge and Experience in the Philosophy of F. C. Bradley*, London, 1964, pp. 147, 148.
37. Ibid.

38. Amos Wilder, 'The Uses of a Theological Criticism', *Soundings: an Interdisciplinary Journal*, No. 1, Spring 1969.
39. Giles B. Gunn, Introduction, *Literature and Religion*, S.C.M., 1971.
40. Robert Conquest, 'Christian Symbolism in *Lucky Jim*', *Critical Quarterly*, Spring 1965.
41. Walter Stein, *Criticism as Dialogue*, Cambridge, 1970.
42. Helen Gardner, *Religion and Literature*, Faber & Faber, 1971.
43. John Osborne, *West of Suez* Faber, 1971.
44. Tzvetan Todorov, 'The Structural Analysis of Narrative', *Novel*, III, 1969, p. 70.
45. Graham Hough, *An Essay on Criticism*, Duckworth, 1967.
46. Runquaya Hasan, 'Rime and Reason in Literature', *Literary Style*, ed. Seymour Chatman, 1971, pp. 309–310.
47. Nathan Scott, 'The Vision and the Poetic Art', *Literature and Belief*, ed. Abrams.
48. D. J. Enwright, 'Beautiful Contradictions', *Encounter*, October 1970, pp. 66, 67.

Chapter Five
1. E. L. Mascall, *Theology and The Gospel of Christ*, S.P.C.K., 1978,
2. George Steiner, 'Whorf, Chomsky, and The Student of Literature', repr. in *On Difficulty and Other Essays*, O.U.P., 1978, p. 156.
3. R. E. C. Browne, *The Ministry of the Word*, S.C.M., 1958.
4. First Epistle of Peter, chapter 2, v. 9.
5. Epistle to the Hebrews, chapter 12, vv. 18, 22.
6. St. John chapter 6, v. 35.
7. St. John chapter 15, v. 1.
8. St. John chapter 14, v. 6.
9. John Bunyan, 'The Author's Apology for his Book', *The Pilgrim's Progress*, pp. 8, 9.
10. St. John chapter 14, v. 9.
11. Epistle to the Hebrews, chapter 1, v. 3.
12. David Lodge, loc. cit. pp. 73ff
13. St. Luke chapter 15, vv. 11–32.
14. J. Moltmann, *The Crucified God*, S.C.M., 1974, p. 245.
15. St. John chapter 1, v. 3.
16. Ephesians chapter 1, v. 23.
17. See above, chapter three, pp. 42, 43, 59.
18. See Lodge, loc. cit., passim.
19. See above, chapter three.
20. See above, chapter four.
21. J. P. Sartre, *What is Literature*, trans. Bernard Frenchman, New York, 1965, p. 37.

Notes

22. Roland Barthes, S/Z, translated Richard Miller, 1975, pp. 5, 6.
23. Lodge, loc. cit., p. 67.
24. J. Heywood Thomas, 'The Problem of Defining a Theology of Culture with Reference to the Theology of Paul Tillich', *Creation, Christ and Culture*, op. cit., p. 287.
25. St. John, chapter 9, v. 39.
26. St. John, chapter 12, v. 48.
27. St. John, chapter 3, v. 19.
28. J. Moltmann, ibid.
29. St. Matthew, chapter 25, vv. 31–46.
30. J. Moltmann, ibid.
31. Karl Barth, ibid.
32. Abhishikta Nanda, *Prayer*, S.P.C.K., 1967.
33. Karl Barth, ibid.
34. David Lodge, op. cit., p. 79.
35. George Steiner, 'After the Book', op. cit., pp. 195, 196.
36. John Osborne, *West of Suez*, Faber 1971, p. 73, 74.
37. Genesis, chapter 11, vv. 1–9.
38. Acts, chapter 2, vv. 1–11.
39. For the context of this, quoted op. cit., No. 884, p. 944, see L. MacNeice, *Collected Poems*, Faber, 1966, Canto VII, 'Autumn Sequel'.
40. A. M. Ramsey, *The Glory of God and the Transfiguration of Christ*, Longmans.